PROTECTING CAPITALISM

CASE BY CASE

ELIOT SPITZER

PROTECTING CAPITALISM

CASE BY CASE

ACKNOWLEDGMENTS

This book is dedicated to the men and women with whom I have served in government. Their enormous wisdom, professionalism, and public spirit set the highest standard and inspired me. I mention only two by name: the Honorable Robert W. Sweet and the Honorable Robert M. Morgenthau.

CONTENTS

4

FIDUCIARY RULES 67

5

CORPORATE GOVERNANCE 84

6

UNDERSTANDING WALL STREET 107

INTRODUCTION

B e careful, we have powerful friends." This wasn't a mob boss speaking to a rival mobster; it was a seasoned, well-respected lawyer for
Merrill Lynch warning me explicitly not to charge his client with major and systemic frauds—the type that destroyed our economy. It was
threats like this, both explicit and implicit, that had kept others from
filing charges.

I laughed at him. "*Now* you tell me," I said. "And what do you expect
me to do now that I know you have powerful friends?" I asked him. We
filed the case the next business day.

In my eight years at Attorney General, and then slightly over one as
Governor, I rode a rollercoaster that took me close to the top of American politics and finance, permitting me to play in the major leagues of
government and economic policy in ways that were as exhilarating and
treacherous as one might imagine from a movie script. I was placed on a
pedestal by some—acclaimed as the Crusader of the Year by *Time* magazine—elected the Governor of New York by an overwhelming majority.

Yet at the same time I was reviled by others—in particular those on
Wall Street—and seen by some as the enemy of all for which capitalism
and our nation stood.

As Icarus, who both rose too quickly and fell precipitously as a consequence, so too did my life crash back from the heights to which I had
ascended. As a result of personal failings that I have neither denied nor
excused, I sacrificed the chance I might have had as Governor to pursue the larger reforms I cared so deeply about. I gave away a life's dream
of following in the footsteps of those great actors whose decisions,
thoughts, and fortitude can in fact alter the course of states.

Yet this book is not about the travails of a personal life, nor a daily diary of calls made and conversations had. Rather, it is meant to be a statement about how we should really understand our economy—as taught by lessons that emerge from cases I brought as Attorney General. I hope these lessons are more subtle, textured, and genuine than the sterile debates of the cable news cycle. And I hope to create a defense of capitalism—and of politics—an argument for people to participate and make ourselves better.

Yes, a defense of capitalism. Because I believe that those who seek to protect and enforce the rules of capitalism are the true supporters and guarantors of capitalism. One has to understand the system—how it works, when it fails, how it actually generates wealth, and for whom—in order to run and manage it effectively. An uncomfortable reality must now be acknowledged: that the image of capitalism propounded by plutocrats who knew how to accrete wealth, too often only for themselves, while breaching fundamental principles and creating almost unlimited long-term costs to society was a poor caricature of capitalism—and a dangerous one.

Using the cases I prosecuted and actions I took in government, I hope to shed light on how we should truly understand capitalism. This book is meant to be a narrative that restores faith in a system that, when properly understood, can be appreciated for what it is and what it does. The warts, flaws, and fissures of the system—as made so evident both by the crises of the past decade and the cases we made—are the windows that permit a true understanding of capitalism.

As with so many things in life, more is learned by losing than winning. So in this book I will tell stories for the purpose of elucidating principles that are visible through the prism of flaws and failure.

This book is also a defense of the necessary role of government. An understanding of how markets actually function and how they must be controlled and buttressed necessarily requires that we appreciate what governments do. The politics that accompanies governance can be ugly—as ugly as the frauds and breaches committed in pursuit of raw profit. Indeed, I have often felt that the blood sport of politics is even uglier than that of finance: Because while business in theory permits an ever increasing pie that can be distributed, it is a reality of politics that power is a zero sum game. And zero sum games are more bitterly fought. Yet this book is in fact a defense of government—the indispensable role it plays in setting and enforcing rules, defining our social contract, investing, and laying the foundation for our successes.

What is so sorely missing right now in our nation is an accepted covenant—an accepted social contract, an accepted articulation of what government is and should be, what the rules of the market are and should be, and what each of us can expect and demand of ourselves and our community. The very social fabric of our nation is being tested.

In a moment of hubris several years back, we believed that our model of capitalism and liberal democracy was the culmination of all ideological development—a neo-liberal take on Francis Fukuyama's "end of history." But we have since seen the collapse of our ideological arrogance, the self-confidence that our model of "free market" capitalism was impervious to challenge or systemic failure. Alternatives have emerged around the world—variations in the model of capitalism, differing legal frameworks. We have seen the greatest destruction of middle-class wealth in U.S. history. We are struggling with a painful reality that our middle class—one of the greatest creations of the last century—is seeing its wealth decay, its income decline, and its confidence in the future evaporate.

As our accepted social contract has shown signs of fraying, self-doubt and anger have replaced confidence as the dominant social sentiment. The sense of renewal that momentarily swept the nation across so many ideological lines with the 2008 election of President Obama has evaporated. Anger and divisiveness have become the driving emotions. The anger that has erupted in our politics—whether that of the Tea Party or Occupy Wall Street—is a consequence of a desperate search for answers.

Twin philosophical battles—John Rawls v. Robert Nozick in the realm of social theory and John Maynard Keynes v. Friedrich Hayek in the realm of economic theory—are playing out in an oscillating, bungee-jump style of politics, with each party sequentially claiming to have categorical answers to seemingly intractable problems. The hard edge apparent in our politics reflects the harsh reality that the ideological battle—while perhaps a constant through our political history—is now superimposed on an economic deterioration that frightens our political discourse, and makes it more harsh.

The challenges of globalization and technology as well have meant that we are no longer placed with ease and absolute certainty at the center of the next century. The unquestioned place of our nation, rooted in our sense of exceptionalism, has been shaken by the past decade. The evocative images of Washington, Hamilton, Jefferson, Lincoln, Teddy and Franklin Roosevelt, Al Smith, Eisenhower, and Reagan no longer breed the comfort and certainty that we will necessarily conquer what lies ahead. And so I write this hoping that the distillation of ideas that emerged over my years in office can in some way be useful to resurrecting the sense of hope and understanding that need to lie beneath a sense of confidence that is rooted in more than self-deception.

I do not intend for this book to be a means of settling scores. Yet while I write with deeper purpose, I would be foolish to believe that I tell the stories from any perspective other than my own. I take full responsibility for characterizations and recollections. I fully recognize that those who disagree will have similar certainty in their views. My purpose in writing is neither the catharsis of confession nor the momentary joy of retribution. It is to try to elucidate and move forward constructively in the policy debate. I recount the material in this book because understanding the historical record permits a more textured understanding of both capitalism and governance.

I have chosen to structure this volume as a series of brief arguments about principles, relying upon cases, prosecutions, and experiences. When I began to articulate some of these principles back in 1999, after being elected Attorney General, much of what I said was viewed as part of an ambition-driven crusade to return to a regulated world that had been overtaken by the iron laws of a new economy. By the aftermath of the crash in 2008, it had become conventional wisdom, and much of it is perhaps now viewed as cliché. But I believe that the thoughts deserve to be heard, internalized, and repeated often. This work succeeds if it reinforces ideas that have now become part of an intellectual framework created by painful experience. Common sense trumps ideology—of the left or the right—every time, and experience teaches that a mixed capitalist system characterized by strong regulation is the only recipe for sensible, sustainable, properly distributed creation of wealth.

Some might properly observe that an individual case or data point does not necessarily prove a generalized principle. However, I think that after observing the past decade of violations in all sectors, we can agree that the cases I discuss here are symptomatic of larger crises, and are not, in fact, isolated examples of defalcation. Greed and dishonesty are the ineluctable moral hazards of capitalism, and a system that fails to recognize and curb excesses is doomed to repeated cycles of boom and bust, with the worst damage falling on those least able to bear it.

In many of the chapters, I have tried to use cases I have prosecuted or issues dealt with from multiple sectors—public, private, and not-for-profit. The behavior we see and have to respond to is not cabined to any one of the major sectors of our economy, and the behavioral issues we have to confront are endemic in all parts of our society. When it comes to our aversion to competition, for instance, despite our claimed dedication to the same concept, I focus on several areas: organized crime, the Gambino family's monopolization of trucking in the garment center; a traditional for-profit business, Marsh & McLennan's illegal bid rigging in the insurance sector; politics, including elected officials' use of gerrymandering to eliminate competition; and education, where the established monopoly schools tried to avoid the competition provided by charter schools. Each of these serves as an example, though in different sectors, of the reality that stands contrary to the commonly taught precepts about how our economy, polity, and society should operate.

I should add that none of these are "my cases." I have been privileged to work with brilliant committed public servants throughout my career, who have inspired me, challenged me, educated me, and supported me, from Judge Robert Sweet to the legendary District Attorney Robert Morgenthau to the dedicated lawyers who served with me in the Office of the Attorney General, where I spent some of my best and happiest days.

I

COMPETITION

Rule One:

Competition is the key to capitalism—

but companies and others do

everything they can to eliminate it!

C ompetition is the elixir that makes capitalism churn and spin, produce and innovate. The incessant pressure to outperform is what
drives the creative juices that spawn the productivity we all desire and
applaud. It generates the wealth that lifts all boats—though sometimes
just the yachts.

The magic of competition is what has made capitalism survive as
virtually every other system of economic production has faded or disappeared—no matter how deep or momentary their intellectual or political appeal may have been. Communism, socialism, and all the rest
have all but disappeared into the history books as the wonders and
creativity of capitalism has spawned the modern world. And the essential ingredient, the special sauce underlying capitalism, has been
competition.

We know this: We were taught it in civics class, in our introductory
economic treatises, and it makes sense.

Yet here is the dirty little secret: Businesses, and indeed those in many
other sectors, spend vast resources, time, energy, and creativity trying
desperately to avoid competition—to defeat it not by outperforming or
building the proverbial better mousetrap or widget, but by subverting
and destroying it through illegitimate means. They do things antithetical to competition because they think they can get away with it, because
they prefer the world without competition—a world where they are
monopolists.

And that is exactly what we should expect them to do! Eliminating
competition by almost any means in order to increase profits, increase
market share, drive every other market participant into bankruptcy—

no matter the means—is what every player in the market *should* want to do. The market is not for the faint of heart or weak of spirit. Who would invest with someone who didn't have the hunger to dominate, to eliminate the competition? Who would want to invest with someone who only wanted 2 percent market share!

Indeed, since the earliest days of our modern capitalist era, the imperative to be a monopolist and eliminate competition has driven our greatest and most successful business leaders. If competition is the theory, it is more honored in the breach: It is the enemy of the business model embraced by many of our iconic business titans, and is the target of attack from all sides on a constant basis.

This is the lesson of Standard Oil and John D. Rockefeller, of U.S. Steel and Andrew Carnegie, in their various monopolist positions, buttressed by the Trusts of the era. This is how some of the great American fortunes were amassed and assembled. The era of big business that preceded the progressive era established that monopoly power—not competition—was the DNA that led to enormous wealth.

Let me be clear: The desire to be a monopolist is not morally objectionable at a deeper level. Or perhaps at any level. There is no commandment that says "thou shall not be a monopolist." Yet monopoly power is antithetical to competition and genuine capitalism. So if we believe that the first rule of capitalism is competition, we had also better be pretty clear in our understanding that just about the first rule of business is doing everything possible to eliminate that very same competition.

Competition does not emerge or survive organically. It must be nurtured, carefully protected from all sorts of adverse behavior. So if we believe that competition actually produces wealth, jobs, and greater productivity, then the obligation to preserve competition must fall to someone—and that someone is government. It is government that sets the rules of competition and enforces them, joined every now and again by private parties in their own litigation. Without government's defining and enforcing the rules of competition, the market would be defined by monopolies and oligopolies—to the detriment of all. In fact, some say that the deregulatory spasm of the past several decades has left us with just that. (See Barry Lynn's powerful book: *Cornered: The New Monopoly Capitalism and the Economics of Destruction.*)

The lessons of Rockefeller were not lost on many—and by the time this chapter is done, we will have ranged across the public and private sectors; legitimate business and organized crime; politics and public schools—all in an effort to establish a simple proposition: Competition is the elixir of capitalism but the enemy of self-proclaimed capitalists. Nobody really wants to compete, and the ways we have discovered to defeat competition run like a thread through all of these diverse areas.

My window into this reality began with organized crime—prosecuting it when I was a young attorney. Only years later did I see the singularity of purpose that ran through so many diverse arenas: from the Gambino organized crime family, which was structuring a cartel to control trucking in New York's Garment District; to the world's largest insurance broker, Marsh & McLennan, which in conjunction with AIG and other supposedly iconic American companies was rigging bids to eliminate competition in the insurance sector; to Bristol-Myers Squibb, one of the world's leading pharmaceutical companies, which manipulated and abused the patent system to keep a generic drug from competing with the brand name equivalent; to Microsoft, which manhandled the competition to protect its operating system; to politicians gerrymandering their districts to eliminate competition; and to public schools objecting to the nascent competition of charter schools.

The enemy was always the same: competition. At every turn, the effort of businesses big and small, organized crime, and sometimes even government officials, was the same—eliminate competition in order to preserve monopoly power and thereby generate profits and maintain power.

Yet for the public at large, what we needed was equally clear: real competition, to eliminate the rot of stagnation. The status quo is often the enemy of progress, yet the status quo is among the most powerful forces we will ever encounter. Change is hard—just as is ensuring the competition that we need to effectuate change.

THE GAMBINO FAMILY AND TRUCKING:

MICHAEL CORLEONE IN REAL LIFE

For me, the saga began in 1988, when I was a mere four years out of law school. Immediately upon graduating from law school, I clerked for one of the great individuals I have had the chance to work with, U.S. District Judge Robert W. Sweet. I then spent a year as an associate at Paul Weiss, where I had the opportunity to work for Arthur Liman, one of the wisest lawyers of his era. It didn't take long, however, before I decided that working as a prosecutor for a few years would be more emotionally satisfying. So on the advice and recommendation of Liman, I joined the office of the legendary Robert Morgenthau.

I was assigned to the "Career Criminal" bureau, where we prosecuted only recidivist violent felons. Their rap sheets were grisly to read, and we were supposed to bring resources and prosecutorial zeal to getting these uniquely violent criminals off the street. My first trial—which I dubbed my "Trading Places" case in honor of the Eddie Murphy movie—led to the conviction of a rather sad figure who pretended to be blind: He used a walking stick as he slowly moved down the street, only to suddenly grab the purse of an innocent bystander and then run off. In the case I prosecuted, he was found, after a minimal chase, with the walking stick hidden in his pants leg. I took great pride in winning this case, but I suppose there would have been greater shame in losing it.

After about a year in the Career Criminal bureau, I was reassigned to the Rackets bureau, whose jurisdiction was political corruption and organized crime. It was, I suppose, the pinnacle of the office: big cases that got the attention of the eighth floor (Morgenthau's office).

Not long after getting there, Mike Cherkasky, the bureau chief and my boss, came into my office—a tiny space that had once been an elevator shaft—and said that the Gambino family controls trucking, and "Let's prosecute them." "So what do we know about it?" I asked innocently, presuming that an investigation had already been done. The answer: You figure it out.

We began with just about that much. Sure, there were typical FBI and NYPD surveillance shots of well-dressed men whispering to each other. But it amounted to nothing. Not a theory, not a fact, and surely not a crime.

What did exist was a wonderful series of articles by a journalist, Tony DeStefano, who had traced the ownership of the four major trucking companies in the Garment District—Lucky, AAA, IMC, and Consolidated—back to individuals alleged to be associated with each of the major organized crime families. And the figure who mattered most was clear: Tommy Gambino, son of Carlo Gambino. If ever there was a real "Capo di tutti capi"—boss of bosses—it had been Carlo. Even after Carlo's demise, when Paul Castellano and then John Gotti took over the title of boss of the Gambino family, Carlo's son Tommy was presumed to be the brains behind the continuing operation of the Gambino family. He didn't have—and didn't want—the glitz of John Gotti. Rather, he was the brains: the smart son who might not even have wanted to be in the mob, but had no choice. He was the real-life Michael Corleone, who in "The Godfather" says so poignantly: "Just when I thought I was out... they pull me back in."

Over the next two years I got to know Tommy Gambino quite well, from listening to thousands of hours of audio tapes, reading hundreds of surveillance reports, and sitting next to him for weeks in a courtroom. In fact, Tommy was much more interested in being part of the Upper East Side of Manhattan and sending his kids to the best schools than he was in spending time in social clubs that were covers for John Gotti's "Goodfellas" world of power and self-importance. Indeed, in an ironic twist of fate, the last time I saw Tommy Gambino, after he had been convicted, and before he was to go to prison, was at Carnegie Hall, enjoying classical music. Sitting in a box in the first tier with my wife, I turned to my left, and there, several rows over, he sat. We saw each other, momentarily processed the remarkably odd nature of this coincidence, nodded slightly, and then went back to appreciating the performance. Truth be told, I kind of liked Tommy Gambino by the time we were done prosecuting him.

The case we brought against Tommy Gambino—and the fact that he was at Carnegie Hall just before entering federal prison—are perfect metaphors for what I call the "white collarization" of traditional organized crime. Organized crime has been a rite of passage for almost every ethnic group that defines New York—Jewish, Irish, Italian, Caribbean, Asian, Russian. We tend to see organized crime through the prism of the Godfather movies, since iconic movies become cultural benchmarks. But in reality, organized crime has at one time or another been controlled by almost every one of the ethnicities that has migrated through New York—which means just about every ethnicity in the world.

As "traditional" OC—the five families—watched the world of business, they concluded that for two critical reasons, leaving loan sharking, drugs, and purely illegal activities to others and shifting their efforts to using illegal means to control legitimate businesses was a better option. First, loan sharking and drugs are by very their nature illegal activities that draw the attention of law enforcement and subject people involved to significant jail time. Whole squads and divisions of major city police departments were focused on just those activities. Second, moving into traditional businesses—meaning legitimate on their face, but running them through cartels or monopolies—is vastly more profitable. It generates more money and is the sort of activity that is usually too complex for law enforcement to examine. Indeed, there is rarely a clear victim; there is no blood on the street, no body calling for immediate law enforcement action. It is better, they rightly decided, to be John D. Rockefeller than a drug kingpin.

And that was Tommy Gambino—the modern mob, the smart mob—running trucking companies in ways that churned out big profits, eliminated all competition, and, until we took a look, probably hadn't attracted a whole lot of law enforcement attention.

The charge Mike Cherkasky gave me, to prosecute the Gambinos, also highlighted a major difference between "street crime"—rapes, robberies, and homicides—and "white-collar crime." With street crime, the fact of a crime is beyond dispute. The victim is screaming for attention, or there is a body on the street. The issue is "who did it?" Gathering the evidence to solve that riddle is the stuff of most law enforcement activity, and most TV dramas about crime.

But white-collar crime begs a more subtle question—*was* there a crime? And if so, what was it? Only after developing a theory of the crime can you even begin to gather evidence to prove it. Watching as all the trucks moved around the Garment District, it surely wasn't so clear that a crime was being committed.

It was only after absorbing the DeStefano articles and doing some reading about the garment industry that I stumbled on an operating theory: This was really a criminal antitrust conspiracy, enforced by the implicit but rarely used threats of beatings and violence. This was the way that NY organized crime had transformed itself—controlling the concrete industry, waste carting, even the fish market. For OC to enforce these cartels, the tentacles of these criminal conspiracies often had to run through major unions, politicians, and even some law enforcement entities. Indeed, the unit within the Rackets Bureau of the DA's office that had been created to focus on these systemic cases was called the "Labor Racketeering unit"—and was designed to focus on the intersection of organized crime, labor officials, and politicians.

Having begun to parse out an operating theory, it was time to figure out how to get evidence. So began a multi-year process of major fits and starts. Initially, we planted an undercover agent on the loading docks of the Gambinos' major company, Consolidated Trucking, where he had to work long, grueling shifts loading trucks. And we learned absolutely nothing useful. Sure, there was some minor gambling going on, but nothing anybody would care about. Then we decided to start our own sting operation, with an undercover agent running a trucking company.

To understand what we hoped to learn by doing this, I have to briefly explain the garment industry. Major design houses that own the labels you see in big stores employ manufacturers to produce the clothing. These manufacturers used to be concentrated in NYC, but now only a few are; most have migrated overseas. Those few that are still in NYC are arrayed—or were in the late '90s—in Chinatown and parts of Brooklyn, with a few still in Midtown. "Piece goods," the actual pieces of fabric that are sewn together into a garment, are shipped from cutting shops to the manufacturers by trucking companies, and then, after being assembled, shipped by these same trucking companies from the manufacturer to a warehouse or the designer's showroom. These truckers controlled the flow of all product—they were the proverbial bottleneck that permitted control of the industry. And just so it is clear: When I use the term "manufacturer," I mean what we would in common parlance refer to as a sweatshop. These sweatshops were stacked in old tenement buildings, 20 to 50 workers arrayed with sewing machines, turning the piece goods into shirts or dresses, attaching buttons and zippers—often working 12-hour days, 6 days a week.

So our second effort, the trucking sting operation, was to have an undercover agent set up a small trucking company and go to every sweatshop in Chinatown seeking work. We offered lower prices, guaranteed delivery. None of it mattered. We got the same response over and over: We are a Consolidated shop—we can't use anybody else. Go away—we don't want trouble. By the time the undercover agent had visited every shop in the region, we had a pretty good map of all the sweatshops in Chinatown and how they were allocated to each trucking company—each controlled by a separate organized crime family. Every sweatshop had one trucker; it knew it; it wouldn't take a chance switching—even for better service or lower cost.

But nobody would tell us of a threat—and nobody even seemed to care that they couldn't choose their trucker. And why should they? They all paid the same inflated price, passed the cost along to the major design or low-end houses for whom they worked, and stayed focused on getting more business. Reducing the cost of their trucking bill simply wasn't a big issue. From their perspective, they were absolutely right to go along with the system. Since all the sweatshops were essentially paying the same tax, nobody cared!

In conversations with the design houses, we got the same response: Of course they knew each sweatshop could use only one trucker, but the cost of trucking was not what they cared about. Everybody knew organized crime was running the trucking companies, but the costs were simply passed along to the consumer. So who was going to fuss? The most we got from any design house was the observation, "But that's Gambino—why would we want to get him upset?" Pretty good logic, frankly.

But in theory someone should care—the truckers who couldn't get business! But who were they, and where? And consumers, too, since they were paying too much—money that went into the pockets of the organized-crime families.

Yet this was the beauty of an antitrust conspiracy: The immediate victims in the business world felt that they were paying the same tax all their competitors paid, and so didn't mind that much. Consumers were not really aware of the scam and had no real recourse anyway; and the only true victims, others who would want to get into the business, were too diffuse or weak to do anything about it.

If our theory was right, there would really be only one way even to gather the evidence: Set up a sweatshop and try to use different truckers. Then we would find out what would happen to us.

So that is what we did. Ronnie Rivera, a state trooper and remarkably talented undercover agent, set up Chrystie Fashions, a real sweatshop on Chrystie Street, in a loft assigned by the trucking cartel to the Gambino's trucking company. We had dozens of workers, probably the only workers in the Garment District actually being paid more than minimum wage and having their taxes withheld. Ronnie, using some pre-existing contacts in the Garment District, actually arranged to get some work. The workers, of course, had no idea the shop was a sting operation designed to gather evidence about the Garment District, and no idea that the small office where Ronnie could look out over the factory floor was wired for sound and video, so we could capture any conversations he would have when the representatives of the Gambinos came by to make sure we were playing by the rules—using only the designated trucker. I wasn't quite sure that overseeing a sweatshop was what I had intended when I went to law school, but this was surely becoming a different type of case.

After producing goods without incident for a couple of months, and using only the Gambino trucks, we decided it was time to push the boundary lines and see what would happen. We put the two sting operations together in order to find out what would happen when we used our own trucker, not the Gambino trucker. And shortly, we got what we had hoped: The Gambino "salesman" came by the shop on his normal visit, checking on our loyalty—and explained the rules to us. Feel free to use your "gypsy" trucker, he told us—gypsy was the phrase in the industry for non-connected non-assigned truckers—as long as you pay us anyway. And to demonstrate his ability to check, the salesman showed us the careful records that he kept of every shipment into and out of every shop. The rule was clear: We control your shop, and we will get paid regardless. And then, just to make sure it was clear, he said: "Don't forget—these are the Gambinos. If somebody doesn't do what they are supposed to, legs will be broken." It was said not so much as a threat, but as a statement of fact.

It is hard to capture the joy in the DA's office when we got this conversation on tape. Our theory was validated! It may not have been quite Hollywood stuff, but the Gambino threat of violence was there to back up the monopoly power of organized crime.

The salesman continued to visit, and we recorded loads of great conversations with him explaining the entire structure of organized-crime control of the Garment District. A gregarious and articulate fellow, he went into great detail about who controlled different operations and what the rules were among the different OC families.

On a more humorous note, reacting one day to a TV drama about organized crime in the Garment District, he said essentially: Can you imagine if anybody ever set up a sting operation in a sweatshop! They could figure all this out! Little did he know he was sitting in the sting operation at that very moment. Sometimes it was hard to separate fiction from reality.

With all this on tape and video, we had the probable cause we needed to get wiretaps for the Gambino offices. The saga of installing those bugs and wiretaps is too far afield from this chapter to get into, but suffice to say that the TV dramas didn't begin to capture all the excitement we saw on that evening. Some amazing work by NY State Troopers—led by the remarkable Dan Wiese—got us where we needed to go.

I spent the next months listening to Tommy Gambino and his brother

Joe for up to 8 hours a day. The amazing thing is that they were actually running a business—making the trucks run on time—and making sure the rules of the conspiracy were enforced: no competition, no poaching, and make sure the sweatshop owners never start to break down the system. But anyone expecting a "Goodfellas" display of vulgarity and violence was listening to the wrong part of the mob.

Indeed, perhaps the best intercept we got had nothing to do with the case. One day Tommy leaned over to Joe—they shared a big desk—and said: "Do you remember what Dad told us?" (Dad, of course, was Carlo Gambino.) I thought we were about to get the holy grail of mob history or wisdom. Where the bodies were buried, who was expected to take over when it was time to pick a new Don. Instead, Tommy said: "You've got to have a Jewish accountant—but you have to watch him!!"

Toward the end of the run of our sweatshop, and having gathered the evidence over the wires that we needed, we orchestrated one final move. Ronnie went to pay a visit to each of the owners of the trucking companies—all organized crime members or associates. In a rather gutsy move, he was wired, and Ronnie went straight into their offices and sought to have them do his trucking, not Consolidated. The uniform response: no way. You know better than that—we don't compete with each other. The sweatshops, they told him, are the property of the trucking companies—and you belong to Consolidated. Moreover, if you violate the rules, we will make sure your work gets cut off.

The rules of the road were clear. The mob ran the trucks, and the rest of us paid. Competition was a nice theory, but let others play by those rules.

Buried in the day-to-day conversations were the meticulous rules of an antitrust conspiracy designed to force every sweatshop and manufacturer to use only the designated trucker, to pay for work not done, to scrape off monopoly profits, and eliminate that critical elixir of capitalism: competition. Indeed, if a shop was sold or leased to a new party, the right to truck all the goods from that shop stayed with the trucking company. Organized crime had a virtual property right in the location. A new shop owner had no right to pick and choose on his own. Because of the monopoly that prevented competition, service was mediocre at best, "gypsies" had to be used to fill in the gaps, and the cost of that was pushed back to consumers. And the opportunity for industrious entrepreneurs who would have otherwise gotten into the trucking business was destroyed.

Having gathered the evidence, overwhelming as it was, we had one problem. This was at its root an antitrust case about preserving competition. The difference between what people expected in a "mob" case and the reality of this one was so vast that there was a real chance people would yawn and not care. Although we dressed the case up with extortion counts that were technically and legally sufficient—and important to understanding the entire fact pattern—the heart of the trial was about proving the intricate rules of the agreement among the trucking companies and the implicit threat that the Gambino family was there to enforce them. In my opening I referred to the Gambinos' use of an "iron hand in a velvet glove"—trying to make it clear to the jury that the actual need for violence would be minimal.

In an odd way, the defense counsel in his opening inadvertently helped me. Gerald Shargel is one of the finest lawyers I have ever encountered. He has charm, grace, wit, a searing intellect—and a scalpel when it comes time to cross-examine. Yet in his opening, he held up a sign with the word "Gambino" in big letters on it. And he argued: If their last name were not Gambino this case would not have been brought. He was right. It was precisely *because* their name was Gambino that they could enforce the conspiracy—everybody did know who they were, what they did, and how they were connected. The Gambino-mob connection wasn't a myth: It was real, as their own "salesman" and the many tapes made clear.

After several long weeks of trial we entered an unusual plea agreement: Based on the record before the jury, it was pretty clear to the lawyers—and probably to Tommy as well as the other defendants—that the efforts of the Gambinos and others to create a monopoly would be proven beyond any doubt. It was also pretty clear to me and the senior lawyers in the DA's office that the traditional "extortion" counts were thin. There really wasn't much need to use threats and violence when the victims of the monopoly could—and did—just pass the costs on to consumers.

So a bargain made sense: The Gambinos would plead guilty to the felony of violating the antitrust laws; we could restructure the industry and restore competition, yet would forgo jail sentences for the defendants. This was the first of what would be many moments in my career when we would struggle with the issue of remedies. (Much more on that in a later chapter) Having proven that something bad had happened, what do you do to fix it? How much do you focus on structural reform as opposed to individual penalties—especially in a white collar as opposed to a violent crime context? (By the way, when I said, in describing our encounter at Carnegie Hall, that Tommy was heading off to jail, he was. He had also been convicted in a subsequent federal case where he had been joined as a defendant with John Gotti.)

What made the Gambino deal an especially difficult decision was that we were dealing with organized-crime defendants and yet our goal was structural reform to the market rather than simply jail time. The terms were pretty straightforward: The defendants pled guilty to a felony, paid a big fine, and got out of the industry. The deal also required that there be a court-supervised monitor who would ensure that organized crime-related individuals would no longer be able to play any role in the garment center, and also ensure that new trucking companies would have access to this lucrative market.

In a front-page *New York Times* article reporting on the deal, Ralph Blumenthal wrote that the case "represented the most ambitious effort ever to dislodge the underworld from control over one of the city's most important industries. ... 'Yes, we gave up jail,' said Robert M. Morgenthau, the Manhattan District Attorney, but he said the agreement accomplished a goal of prosecutors since Thomas E. Dewey and promised to save a 'dying' industry that had lost two-thirds of its jobs over the last 30 years."

One great moment occurred when we were handling the mechanics of the settlement. Pursuant to the plea agreement, Tommy Gambino had cut a check for one million dollars, made out to Kroll Associates, the court-appointed monitor, to cover the initial costs of establishing the industry supervision. Gambino had arranged to have the check delivered. The messenger didn't know that, by pure coincidence, Kroll Associates was in a building where a totally unrelated stationery store—also named Kroll—was located on the ground floor. In error, the messenger took the check to the stationery store. The owner of the store, upon receiving a check for one million dollars from Tommy Gambino—a famous mob figure—didn't know whether to be terrified or overjoyed. In the end it was all sorted out, and the right Kroll got the check.

Not long after the case was resolved, Jerry Shargel and I had lunch at Sparks, a great steak house where John Gotti had arranged for the murder of Paul Castellano, then the head of the Gambino crime family. The crime occurred right in front of the restaurant, as Castellano's car was being parked, and produced photos of bullet-ridden bodies strewn across New York City streets, which were on the cover of every tabloid paper. This was the murder that made Gotti the boss of the Gambino crime family. Shargel had been Gotti's lawyer in multiple criminal prosecutions, including those relating to this murder. Over lunch, Shargel asked slyly if I knew what Gotti had told him about Sparks. I played along and said, No Jerry, please tell me. Jerry said, with a big grin, "The food is great, but parking is murder."

Several years later, Selwyn Raab, a *New York Times* reporter who had covered OC for years, went back to take a look at the garment trucking industry. He asked a simple question: Had the effort to restructure the industry worked? Was there competition, or had the same system of allocating sweatshops to one trucker and making consumers pay survived our effort to shake things up? Happily, in a big front-page article, he concluded that we had succeeded in injecting real competition. It is worth quoting some of his analysis:

"Three years after prosecutors claimed they had broken the Mafia's choke hold over vital trucking routes in New York City's garment industry, many manufacturers say that shipping costs have dropped sharply and that dozens of new trucking companies are now competing for business.

"Garment manufacturers estimate that in three years, the average price for shipping a dress, a pair of jeans, or a blouse has plunged to 15 to 20 cents from 40 to 45 cents.

"Prosecutors said the falling costs reflected the demise of a mob cartel that had inflated prices and milked customers for half a century....

Mr. [Thomas] Wong, the owner of T and L Fashions at 129 Lafayette Street in lower Manhattan, said that before the court order, he had no choice in truckers. Nor could he negotiate prices.

"'Once the shop belonged to a trucker, you could not use any other,' he asserted. 'There were no physical threats. But if they found out you used someone else, the bottom line was you had to pay them anyway to get off the hook.'"

At the time we cut the deal with the Gambinos, there had been the predictable, and in fact justifiable, questioning about the deal we had cut. Would it work? Was it the right remedy in a criminal case? Was it the place of government to try to reshape the market? These questions were a precursor of the same questions I would face over the years I was AG as we tried to remedy even deeper structural problems in other markets. Perhaps because of our success in the trucking case, I was persuaded not only that the government's role in breaking up monopolies and ensuring competition was critical, but also that meaningful resolution of a case like this required creativity. Doing something so that the status quo didn't simply reinvent itself was the key to making a difference. In this case I thought we had.

The court-appointed monitor in the Gambino case, former New York Police Commissioner Robert McGuire, stated it perfectly when he was quoted in the Raab article: "This is a new approach to solving an endemic problem of organized crime infiltration of an industry. Sending one organized-crime figure to jail and having him replaced by another has no long-term effect. This is a systemic attempt to change the fundamental way business is conducted in the garment industry and to level the playing field for all competitors."

I didn't realize that reshaping organized crime practices was easy compared to reshaping Wall Street. That was a lesson I would learn later on.

MARSH MAC:

A COMPANY

WITH THREE BROKEN LEGS

The desire to be a monopolist runs deep—whether for organized-crime families or "traditional" businesses. Competition, after all, is a serious impediment to profit margins. So it was with Marsh & McLennan, the world's biggest insurance broker, and its desire to dominate the insurance industry. Marsh Mac had three primary legs to its structure: the insurance brokerage, Putnam mutual funds, and Mercer consulting. In a bizarre twist of fate, while I was AG we had major and successful investigations relating to every piece of the Marsh structure. Marsh at the time had as its CEO Jeff Greenberg—the son of Hank Greenberg, the now former but then still reigning CEO of AIG. Jeff, who had worked at AIG for a time, seemed intent while at Marsh on proving that he too could become a corporate titan.

Often during the period I was Attorney General I would analogize the behavior of the organized crime families to the behavior of some of our major companies. Needless to say, a lot of people got bent out of shape by that. But there was a reason I made the analogy. As I said above, the organized crime families learned about monopoly power from the history of the oil and other trusts, and traditional businesses learned the power of monopoly the same way. They all decided that the best way to extract profits and ensure a lack of competition was collusion, not competition. Marsh exemplified this.

Marsh Mac was the largest insurance brokerage company in the world—and as we all learn at some point in time, insurance is at the center of almost every transaction. Marsh didn't provide the insurance coverage itself; it was the broker a company would hire to find the best insurance coverage out there. Marsh had as its clients many, if not most, of the major companies in our economy, as well as a whole load of government entities: school boards, towns, cities. Marsh promised its clients that it would be loyal to them as it sought the best insurance package for their needs. So whether it was a school board seeking liability insurance for the potential suits it could face for injuries on its football field, or GE seeking coverage for the failure of an airplane engine, Marsh was supposed, and obligated, to get the best coverage at the best price for its client. (More about these "fiduciary duties" and how often they are violated, in Chapter Four.)

But just as the Gambinos and the other organized crime families divided up the trucking market to ensure there would be no competition, so too did Marsh arrange the market so it could make bigger fees—scraping off profits to which it was not entitled, and which were the product of behavior directly contrary to the principles of integrity and competition in the marketplace.

How did it do this?

Simple: Among its other schemes, it arranged for fake bids, telling the various insurance companies what they should bid in each instance, ensuring that the company it wanted to have the best bid would in fact win. Bids were labeled "A" and "B" bids—"A" bids being real, "B" bids being fake, designed to create the false appearance of competition for the unknowing customers of Marsh. In return for guaranteeing the insurance companies that provided the real and fake bids the additional profit that resulted, because their bid rigging elevated the price at which the insurance was sold, Marsh insisted that these companies then kick back some of these inflated profits to Marsh. They called these payments "contingent fees." A company that didn't put in bids as required would be squeezed; a company that played ball would get more and more business, at a higher price, without needing to face real competition.

And all the while, Marsh would get the kickbacks, through its "contingency fees." Who lost? Marsh's customers—who were supposed to be getting insurance that was the product of competition and honest advice from Marsh. In 2003 alone these contingent fees—kickbacks— amounted to $800 million, more than half of Marsh's net income. The illegality permeated the entire business.

Discovering this "business model" so we could prosecute this case was not nearly as exciting as the Gambino investigation: no sting operations, no undercover work, just a lot of reading of emails.

But the emails were pretty explicit in how the underlying effort was all about killing competition—rigging the market. As one Marsh executive told his subordinates, the size of the contingent commissions to Marsh determined "who [we] are steering business to and who we are steering business from." (Complaint in People of the State of New York v. Marsh & McLennan, filed October 4, 2004.)

The complaint we filed against Marsh laid out a companywide scheme and was accompanied by criminal cases against several executives. The facts presented made it manifest that the loyalty to the customer and dedication to competition that were supposed to guide their business were totally absent. One vignette, set out in the complaint, recounts a typical instance in which Marsh asked ACE, a major insurance company, to *increase* the price on its bid, to ensure that AIG would keep the business. Marsh was increasing the cost to its client so it could direct business and extract illegal kickbacks. As an internal ACE email explaining the increase in the bid price stated: "We were more competitive than AIG in price and terms. [Marsh] requested we increase premium to $1.1M to be less competitive, so AIG does not loose [sic] the business."

After the civil complaint and the criminal cases were announced, I stated that I could not negotiate with the CEO, Jeff Greenberg, who, in our meetings and accompanied by counsel, had simply refused even to acknowledge that collusion, false bids, and bid rigging were illegal and wrong. Not surprisingly, the board of Marsh, which had until then been fully responsive to Greenberg's wishes, replaced him. But much to the surprise of many, including me, they replaced him with a friend of mine: Mike Cherkasky, who had been my boss when I was making the Gambino case! He had run Kroll, the investigation company, and later a division of Marsh, and now, at their request, stepped in as CEO of the parent company.

If they thought they would catch a break by bringing in Mike, they were wrong. We negotiated an $850 million settlement—most of it going into a fund that would provide restitution to the victims of the Marsh fraud. Just as important, the company admitted to the illegal behavior, saying: "The recent admissions by former employees of Marsh and other companies have made clear that certain Marsh employees unlawfully deceived their customers."

And at a structural level, just as we had in the Gambino context, we demanded changes to the underlying business practices: We required that contingent commissions and the entire structure of kickbacks be eliminated.

The number of companies involved in this scheme was vast, both in terms of the volume of insurance sold and also in terms of market share: Each of the three largest insurance brokers and many of the largest insurance carriers were implicated.

Why does this matter? Because again the underlying point here is not about contingent commissions; it is about the degree to which anti-competitive behavior had permeated one of the central and most critical pathways of commerce. The companies, seeing the opportunity to increase profits, colluded, just as Rockefeller had, and just as the Gambinos had.

At the end of the day, when we arranged for $850 million to be returned and the structure of insurance sales to be altered, we were trying to do the same thing we had done with the Gambinos and trucking: restore competition and stop the behavior of those who, through threats—implicit or explicit—or simply by using sham bids, could eliminate the tonic of competition and keep for themselves all the upside. Marsh and the Gambinos were trying to do the same thing. And until we, through government intervention, stopped them, nothing in the marketplace alone would have.

Oddly, the biggest beneficiaries of the Marsh settlement were major companies. Since Marsh had been a brokerage that had as its primary client base other major corporations, these major companies were the ones that benefited most when money was returned. My recollection is that GE got the single biggest check—many millions of dollars. Restoring competition wasn't just a populist crusade. The biggest players themselves were going to win as well. Indeed, it perhaps wasn't until we did the "mutual fund cases"—much more about those in a later chapter—that the returns really flowed directly to smaller investors and players in the market.

BIG PHARMA AND GENERICS:

ANOTHER TALE

OF SUPPRESSING COMPETITION

Let's move from the worlds of organized crime and insurance to another enormous sector in our economy—the pharmaceutical companies—because the imperative to eliminate competition drove big pharma to break the rules as well. And still does.

We all know that pharma—everyone from the major companies to the smaller biotech startups—invests a lot of money developing the miracle drugs that cure us. In return they are given patent rights, so that for many years the company that controls the patent is permitted to have a monopoly. This is a societal trade-off. It is one of the rare instances where we permit and even encourage a monopoly. Whatever sins may be committed by the companies in their abuse of monopoly power, we surely must feel gratitude toward the wizards who develop the marvelous drugs that cure us. So in order to induce the enormous investment and risk involved in research and development, we give the pharma companies the right to make the often extraordinary profits that can be generated by having a monopoly in a drug that cures an awful disease—for a defined period of time.

However, once that time period runs out, there is supposed to be competition, and other drug companies are allowed to market alternative products that often use identical science. These are often marketed as generic drugs and are the chemical equivalent of the original drug. This serves to drive the price down substantially.

The company that developed the original drug, needless to say, has a big incentive to keep generics off the market. And so the saga of Bristol Myers-Squibb (BSM) and Taxol. The details of both the technology and the patent law are too gnarly to try to repeat here, but let me reduce it to this: Taxol, a highly profitable and expensive drug manufactured by BSM to treat breast and ovarian cancer, was protected from competition from generics for five years. As the end of the five-year period approached, BSM illegally tried to obtain patents that would block generic

competition, by deliberately misrepresenting the state of scientific research to the patent office, fraudulently obtaining two patents based on
those misrepresentations, and then abusing those patents to stop competitors from entering the marketplace. BSM used a similar approach to
extend its monopoly on BuSpar, an anti-anxiety drug.

As a result, in the case of Taxol in 2002, and BuSpar in 2001, we filed
suit against BSM. In 2003, BSM settled and agreed to disgorge about
$670 million, about the amount of profit it had made from its illegal
behavior.

Lest you think this sort of effort by big pharma has been stopped, just
recently it was announced that British authorities had accused GlaxoS-
mithKline, another major pharma company, of simply paying off a potential generic competitor to stop it from bringing a product to market.
This behavior has long been viewed by most prosecutors and antitrust
experts as violative of the law, a position just embraced by the U.S. Supreme Court.

Big pharma's effort to maintain illegal monopoly power has been both
creative and enormously harmful to consumers, and to the legitimate
functioning of the marketplace.

Of course, the biggest antitrust case in recent years was probably the
case brought against Microsoft by the state Attorneys General, which
the Department of Justice later joined. This case was initiated before I
became Attorney General in 1999, and it probably establishes a different
lesson: In a sector as rapidly evolving as tech and computers, monopolists are more likely to fall prey to new technology than to government
prosecution. That doesn't mean the prosecution was wrong or ill con-
ceived. It just means that in the fast-changing tech sector, new technologies are more likely to succeed in breaking down monopoly power
than anything put in place by government through the slow, laborious
process of litigation. Although we negotiated a good resolution to the
case, the advent of new operating systems did more to limit Microsoft's
power than did the litigation.

MONOPOLY POWER

IN POLITICS

L et's change directions for a moment. We have seen the same thread
run through organized crime and trucking, insurance, pharmaceuticals, computers and operating systems. The theory is applicable to
government as well.

How do elected officials try to maintain their own monopoly? They try
to rig elections. Now I don't mean stuffing the ballot box—that would be
too crass. Of course it did used to happen, and maybe it still does on

rare occasion. But more subtle methods exist. By drawing district lines that prevent real competition, we might as well be doing the same thing. What we call gerrymandering is the political equivalent of what Marsh did when it rigged the bids, or what the Gambinos did when they didn't permit any other truckers to seek their customers. We say to the other party: You can put up a candidate, but we all know that you can't win in this district, because we have drawn the lines in such a way that a Republican can never win. And in return for your letting me win this one, I'll make sure we don't really compete in the district over there on the other side of town.

Gerrymandering is the political equivalent of an antitrust conspiracy forged by two political parties to ensure that they keep control of their part of the market. And who suffers? The public—because we don't get the benefit of hard-fought competition and the elevated performance and political discourse that would theoretically result. The lack of competition in legislative elections, by the way, also has bred the increasing divisiveness in Congress, and contributed substantially to the levels of corruption in statehouses. The lack of competition creates an atmosphere of inviolability that permits illegal conduct and a lack of scrutiny.

And unfortunately, just as there has been little or no enforcement of the rules of competition in the private sector, so too with respect to the political arena, the Supreme Court has permitted the rules of competition to be diluted. State legislatures, which determine the boundaries of Congressional borders and their own legislative boundaries, have been given way too much latitude to preserve the monopoly of the parties. Gerrymandering is to politics what abuse of monopoly power is to the economy at large. And permitting one is no more legitimate than permitting the other.

Let's try a different area of the public sector: schools. Public schools essentially have a monopoly as well. They provide the service we need, but there is virtually no competition in the public sector. Sure, there are high-priced private schools, and in some cities parochial schools that cost less but still charge a fair bit. But there is usually no competition accessible to most parents within the realm of public schools. At least there really wasn't until charter schools popped up. I don't want to wade into the enormous debate that is rightly going on right now about whether charter schools outperform traditional public schools or not. But I do know that by providing competition and a reference point that didn't exist in a monopoly context before they were there, charter schools have given parents the opportunity to see the benefits of competition. Parents have been able to go to the traditional public schools and say hey, if they are doing that, why can't you? So even when charter schools are limited in number—sometimes only a very small percentage of the students attend in any given community—that might be enough to provide the competitive spirit that lifts all performances, or at least demonstrates what can be done, sufficient to stimulate parents and others to demand that other schools do more. That is why when I was Governor I doubled the number of charter schools in New York State.

Competition really is the elixir that makes capitalism or any system of production work. We need the benefits of competition in all the diverse sectors of the economy. Yet the desire to avoid competition is equally powerful. Organized crime tries desperately to run monopolies; so do Marsh, big pharma, our elected officials, and our schools.

So what does all this mean? How are we to respond? Only when a really tough government can step in to ensure that competition is restored will that elixir that we truly believe is the key to markets actually come back into the picture. Those of us who have argued for government intervention in defense of competition are often derided as not understanding "the market." A school of thought evolved—supported by the conservative Heritage Foundation, the Chamber of Commerce, and the writings of Judge Bork—that those of us who brought antitrust actions were the ones acting contrary to capitalist theory. Those voices could not have been more wrong, and they continue to be wrong. We are the ones who believe in the elixir of competition, and are willing to stand up to the enormous pressures that are brought to bear by market participants to destroy it. If you believe in competition—and are willing to fight for it—prepare for the slings and arrows of faux capitalists: those who hide behind their false "free market" rhetoric to defend monopolists of all stripes.

2

SUPPLY AND DEMAND

Rule Two:

Supply and demand curves

don't always give us

the right price and quantity.

Nothing is more central to our understanding of markets and capitalism, after the notion of competition itself, than the maxim that supply and demand curves intersect to give us the right quantity and supply of any given product. We have all seen the curves charted out—and the point of intersection labeled "equilibrium"—as though it is a resting spot of perfect comfort. It also seems so intuitive: If the price goes up, more people produce a product, though fewer people will demand it; on the other side, when the price goes down, fewer people will produce the product but more people will want it. When these two curves intersect, we have that magic point of equilibrium—and all is well. It is indeed one of the most recognized charts in the world:

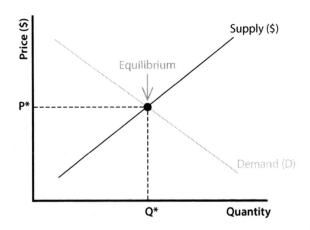

The problem is that this point of perfect equilibrium often doesn't get us the optimal level of supply or demand. It isn't what it pretends to be. And here is why: These curves, as ordinarily drawn, reflect only the interests and desires of the two people participating in the transaction— the people who bid on the price and create the demand, and those who determine whether they are willing to sell and supply the product! How about the interests of the people NOT part of the deal? It could be just one person—a neighbor—or it could be a whole community, or the entire global population! How do the economic impacts on them, positive or negative, get factored in to determine the best level of output from a societal perspective? That is the critical question not answered when we look at the desires only of the people who are party to the deal itself.

How can people not a part of a transaction have any rightful say in what the price or quantity should be? And how can I get away challenging the foundation stone of our understanding of economic theory? To figure this out, let's take an example. What if the price of dirty, high-sulfur coal is very cheap, so that an energy company can produce lots of cheap energy, pleasing its consumers, who get a pretty low utility bill, but as a consequence the utility spews out huge clouds of soot and noxious gases onto the neighboring properties, in an extreme case making these properties uninhabitable and also adding to the problem of greenhouse gases and global warming? Should the economic and non-economic cost of the soot and pollution on the surrounding properties, and on the larger environment, affect the amount of energy from dirty coal that it is best to produce?

Common sense would tell us yes. Just as the noise from a neighbor's party makes an apartment less desirable, so too does the coal's pollution diminish the value and desirability of an entire neighborhood or region, creating an economic impact—as well as a social one—that should be factored into our model. And of course, unlike the noise from a party that will end at some point, the pollution from the coal might have long-term devastating environmental impacts.

The costs—there can, of course, be benefits as well—that accrue to people who are NOT party to the actual transactions are called "externalities" by economists. And the fact of these externalities *should* in fact be part of the equation when we determine the amount of any given product that we produce—and the price at which it is sold. Yet the cost or benefit of these externalities is NOT reflected in the supply and demand curves that private parties see and react to, unless government does something to regulate the market. The "somethings" can be a tax on a product, increasing the price of the product and so diminishing the level of output; or a rule about how you produce it, effectively reducing the level of the output of the pollution; or a limit on where it can be produced, so the geographic impact is limited in a way that reduces social costs. Or, on the other side, if we want to increase production of something that has positive externalities, government can put in place a subsidy designed to increase the level of production.

Even the most conservative economists out there agree with this statement of theory and principle. It is because of "negative externalities" that we tax polluters; it is because of "positive externalities" that we subsidize research and development. It is because smoking has negative externalities—it increases the level of cancer and raises health costs for all of society—that all economists agree that taxing smoking is a legitimate and smart thing to do. It is because education has positive externalities for all of society—beyond the mere benefits to the person being educated—generating economic growth and a more learned society at large, that we subsidize education.

So never again agree with someone who says simply, "Well, that is the price that the market set, and the quantity the market set, and therefore it must be right." Wrong! Unless the supply and demand curves are modified to reflect the cost or benefit of these externalities, the market is setting the wrong price and quantity. And in fact, that is why the "market" very often doesn't get it right.

Now whether it makes sense in every instance, or any, to try to factor in these positive or negative externalities is a difficult analysis: The cost, difficulty, and sometimes near impossibility of measuring the externalities need to be factored into any decision. But the theory that the proper price and volume of output cannot be set without considering them is crystal clear, and the reality that there are also times when the magnitude of the externalities calls for some market intervention is also crystal clear.

So let me tell you a story. When I was Attorney General I was asked to testify before a U.S. Senate committee about several lawsuits the New York Attorney General's office had brought against some power companies in Ohio to enforce the Clean Air Act—one of the most important environmental statutes on the books. Parenthetically, the Clean Air Act was signed into law by President Nixon, hardly a liberal. When I was testifying, Ohio's Sen. George Voinovich, who had been the Governor of Ohio before being elected Senator, looked down from the dais and said, with some element of pride and grandeur, words to the effect of "General Spitzer, when I was the Governor of Ohio we cleaned up the air in Ohio, so why are you now suing the power companies in my state?"

My answer went something like this: "Senator, I applaud you for having cleaned up the air in Ohio, but do you remember how you did it? You had the power companies build big, tall smokestacks—over 1,000 feet tall. They didn't build them that tall because it was cheap, or because they were pretty. They did it because that way when they burned cheap dirty coal, the soot and smog went way up in the air, up into the jet stream, and it didn't come down in Ohio. It didn't even come down in Pennsylvania or New Jersey. You got cheap energy and clean air. And I applaud you for that. But here's the problem. That soot and smog, and the acid rain that it caused, came down in New York! We didn't get cheap energy; we just got dirty air and bad health. So I am going to do what lawyers do: Sue the power companies to make sure OUR interests are protected."

Now why the power companies were violating the Clean Air Act, and why the law was designed the way it was so we could vindicate the rights of all the folks downwind of the Ohio power plants, is something we will get to in a moment. The key point here is that the Ohio power companies were shifting the burden of their production—the cost of the pollution—to people who weren't even part of the transaction. That is a perfect example of an externality. Ohio consumers got cheap power, the Ohio utility got good prices and healthy profits because it could sell its product pretty cheaply, but New Yorkers got the pollution! People not party to the transaction had no say in how much was produced, or at what price. Since the cost to society of the pollution wasn't reflected in the supply and demand curves determining how much power was produced in Ohio, too much dirty coal and smog was being produced. If the true cost of the product, including the cost of the smog and acid rain, had been reflected in the supply and demand curves, then and only then would the market have set the right price and quantity. And that is what we were trying to do by bringing the suit: make sure the costs to New Yorkers were reflected in the decision. No serious economist would dispute this analysis.

This is not an isolated example. Take the case of noxious odors. Imagine that someone decided to place a fish market right in the middle of a residential community. On a hot summer day that wouldn't be so appealing. The smell would have a pretty negative impact on the livability of the community and the value of the homes. Simply looking at the price the vendor would pay for the real estate and concluding that the market had set the right price would be wrong from a societal point of view. That is one reason we have zoning rules—to protect neighbors from the externalized impact of differing types of behavior. Zoning laws are really absolute bars to some types of behavior: manufacturing in a residential community, for instance. This is one way of saying that having the supply and demand curves intersect where private parties alone might set them doesn't always get to the right result.

Realize that these externalities can often be positive as well—meaning we want more of something than the price set by the market—because people who are not part of the transaction actually benefit. And so we subsidize the product. One such product is research and development. The results are so beneficial to society that we encourage basic research and development because the parties to the transaction themselves might not generate enough of it otherwise. Think about the role that the National Institutes for Health plays in supporting research. Because private parties, for instance the major pharmaceutical companies and the major educational institutions, can't capture enough of the profits from basic research, they don't invest as much in that area as we think society requires. Or think about the spinoffs that NASA has contributed to scientific advancement. That really is a form of government's subsidizing scientific research in areas where the private sector alone, or private parties alone, might not have either seen or been able to capture all the upside. So society wants more basic R&D, and we subsidize it—by giving grants to universities or big pharma, or by having government do the research itself.

Externalities are one form of what we call "market failures," instances where the simple intersection of supply and demand curves do not get us to the right quantity of output at the right price. There are many other forms of "market failure," but we won't get into them right now.

So when we began suing power companies to get them to comply with the Clean Air Act, this was the economic reason. If we truly wanted to get the price and quantity of energy that reflected the interests and total costs to society, our lawsuits and the remedies they sought had to be brought. Let me tell you the story.

SUING THE POWER COMPANIES:

DON'T SEND US YOUR SOOT WHEN

YOU KEEP THE JUICE!

When I became AG in 1999, one of the cases I inherited was a lawsuit against the EPA, which sought to compel the EPA to lower pollution limits in states upwind of NY—which means their pollution came to NY. Over three-quarters of the air pollution in most parts of NY comes from upwind states, so nothing we did inside the state would adequately clean our air. The Clean Air Act requires the EPA to address this problem by limiting pollution in upwind states, but politics had proven to be an insurmountable barrier. Regardless of the political party controlling the White House, the EPA had failed to act. So NY had sued the EPA. But this case promised to move very slowly, and even judicial success was likely to prove ineffective in getting what we really needed: reduced pollution. Clearly, we needed a new approach.

Peter Lehner, whom I had brought in as a new chief of the environmental bureau, came to me with an idea: Why don't we sue the upwind coal-fired power plants directly—the ones responsible for pollution that was killing over 10,000 Americans each year—rather than wait for the EPA to act? Force the power companies to abide by the law and stop polluting!

A short note about Peter: When I was looking for a chief of the environmental bureau, after being elected, we got a slew of good résumés. But none was perfect. The one common theme in all the good résumés was that they had Peter Lehner as a reference. Clearly he was the guy everybody in the area thought was best. So we reached out to him, and worked hard to persuade him to come on board. It was one of the best recruitment decisions I made.

The legal and factual backdrop in our cases against the power plants is actually not that complicated. Under the CAA, the Clean Air Act, *new* power plants had to have state-of-the-art pollution controls that would reduce smog and soot causing pollution by 85 to 95 percent. But old power plants were protected; they were grandfathered in and did not need to install the expensive pollution controls, *unless they modified their plants*, in which case they were treated like new plants. As the economy grew, few new plants had been built, so Peter wondered where the new electricity had come from. We went out and dug into the volumes of filings made by the energy companies throughout the Midwest. We found that many coal-fired power plants had in fact upgraded or modernized their plants—substantially increasing their output—but *without* installing the required pollution controls.

The power companies avoided the law by falsely claiming that the upgrades, costing tens of millions of dollars, were "routine maintenance." These actions, we believed, violated the new source review provisions of the CAA, and the State of New York could sue these plants directly, requiring them to put in the environmental controls mandated by the statute.

It sounded like a great idea to me, so I authorized Peter to do all the research and preparation for the suits. We invited the NYS Department of Environmental Conservation to join us as plaintiffs, but they declined to do so. It was one of many instances where the regulatory agencies who should have been our partners were too squeamish to actually require that people abide by the terms of the law.

There was also a perception problem we had to deal with. We were worried that the upwind polluters we were planning to sue would claim that NY was simply trying to get a competitive advantage by making upwind state electricity more expensive (it was already much less expensive than electricity in NYS). If all we did was sue non-NY plants and ignore pollution generated within our own state, they would have had a good case on that point. So we realized that while NYS plants were much smaller, they also contributed to air pollution, and many had violated the same law. So we developed cases against all the NYS coal-fired power plants that had also used the "routine maintenance" argument improperly. We needed to show we were enforcing the law fairly against all polluters, not just targeting non-NYS plants.

Finally, we agreed that it would help to have other states come along with NY, so we brought the AG's of Connecticut and New Jersey into our plans. It is critical to note that while I and the AG of Connecticut, Richard Blumenthal, now a U.S. Senator, were independently elected and Democrats, the AG of NJ was appointed by the Governor—in this case the Republican Christie Todd Whitman. These were bipartisan cases. Don't miss the symbolism here: Gov. Whitman joined us. Yet several years later, when she was the head of EPA under President George W. Bush, she had to change directions, as the Bush Administration undercut our enforcement effort.

In September 1999, we announced that we would sue 51 power plants owned by a half-dozen different companies. Under the CAA, a person suing must give notice to the polluter, the EPA, and the state in which the polluter is located, 60 days before filing the suit. During the next 60 days a flurry of negotiations ensued, but none reached fruition. The good news, however, was that the federal Department of Justice, which had been investigating similar claims but had been under great Congressional pressure not to act on them, was now able to move forward. They joined NYS in almost all of our cases.

These cases lasted many years and a whole book could be written just about them. It is not an exaggeration to say that they completely changed the discussion about air pollution and coal-fired power plants. We went to trial against Ohio Edison and the judge agreed with us that the company had violated the law. We then were able to settle with them and several other companies. In total, the companies agreed to install pollution controls worth over $8 billion, pay penalties and support supplemental projects of several hundreds of millions of dollars, and reduce pollution by over a million tons of emissions a year. These cases saved thousands of lives. The cases also led to pressure to address soot and smog pollution more broadly, by new EPA regulations, which, although they have been bogged down in court challenges, promise to save even more lives. In the end, we filed multiple suits, leading to a multitude of settlements requiring that many billions of dollars be spent on environmental upgrades, and millions of tons of carbon dioxide and nitrogen oxide not being discharged into the environment.

The cases also highlighted the role of coal and its political power. When President Bush came into office, one of the first things he did was to ask Vice President Dick Cheney to lead a task force on energy. It met scores of times with power companies and almost never with health or environmental experts. The result, especially given the tremendous amount of money the coal and power companies had poured into Bush's campaign, was no surprise. The President urged Congress to repeal the provision of the CAA we were enforcing, and he had his EPA try to re-write the rules we were relying on. So in addition to continuing the cases against the polluters, we had to repeatedly sue the Bush EPA for itself violating the CAA with its new rules. And despite the deference federal courts usually give to federal agencies, we usually won those cases. (In-deed, in other areas of environmental law, the same thing happened, with the Bush EPA trying to promulgate rules that were far weaker than Congress had demanded in the underlying law. We sued the federal gov-ernment over three dozen times, often with a large coalition of other states, and won most of those cases.)

In the end, these cases also became a model as other states realized that they could and should take a more active role in enforcing pollution safeguards. We and others brought cases to protect water quality, public health, wildlife, and our communities.

Perhaps just as important, these cases demonstrated the critical fact that because of "market failures" that we call externalities, government action was necessary to get us to the right point of supply and output for everything from energy to basic research. Enforcement of the regula-tions that the "free market" voices loved to mock was not antithetical to the way the market was supposed to function. In fact, it was critical to making it work properly.

INVESTIGATING CAPITAL MARKETS

AS A CIVIL RIGHTS ISSUE

Let me suggest another type of negative externality, one that is not viewed this way too often, but should have been: too much debt in our economy. We all know that too much debt and grotesque levels of leverage were two of the major factors leading to the cataclysm of 2008. And the government entities that should have been there to stop the ac-cretion of debt and leverage along the way failed utterly to do anything. Their response was: The market is factoring the debt into the evaluation of credit ratings, and interest rates will rise if there is too much debt, limiting borrowing. Put aside the failure of integrity in the ratings and issuance of debt—and more about that later on—the government agen-cies failed even to understand conceptually that too much debt could metastasize and do enormous harm to the macro economy. Each bor-rower, or each bank in issuing the debt, loan by loan, failed to realize that the aggregate level of debt was creating a negative externality. The compounding effect would do great harm that no individual lender or borrower could see.

One bad subprime loan may be harmful to the parties involved, but is not dangerous to the economy writ large. Yet an entire industry spewing out bad debt would harm not just the individuals involved in the transaction, but, at the end of the day, the entire economy. When all the securitized debt fails at once, the negative externality can destroy our economy—as it did in 2008. That is why wiser regulators at the Office of the Comptroller of the Currency, the Federal Reserve Board, and elsewhere, would have stepped in much earlier to lower leverage ratios, ensure the quality of loans that were being made and securitized, and lend stability to our capital markets. Of course, the regulators, by and large, totally missed the larger picture. My window into this world began with our first investigation of subprime debt—all the way back in 1999.

When I became Attorney General, one of the things that I cared about was that financial markets—everything from trading in stocks and bonds, to small business lending—operated fairly and in a way that was accessible to all. Motivated in part by my dad's stories about the importance of access to capital as a basic piece of success, that concern played out in a very particular way in the civil rights context. I remember telling my civil rights team, even before I took the oath of office, that we needed to be on the lookout for cases where banks refused to lend to people living in minority neighborhoods. It's a practice known as "redlining," so called because, as far back as the 1920s, some banks actually drew red lines on the maps showing the border between mostly white neighborhoods and predominantly minority ones. On the "white" side of the red line, banks were happy to lend money at reasonable rates; on the "minority" side, credit was simply unavailable. It was a subtle but devastating form of Jim Crow, and it was certainly not limited to the South. Access to capital was the key to success in the American system. Without it, starting or growing a new business, even buying a home, was extremely difficult.

So "access to capital" became a watchword. Minority neighborhoods needed more capital, we believed. If banks were denying credit to people on illegitimate grounds—race, creed, or any other suspect classification—we would go after them, hammer and tong.

I wasn't in office three weeks before word of possible lending discrimination landed on my desk—on the front page of *The New York Times* Metropolitan section. It was an article about a mortgage lending company that, advocates said, was victimizing African-American homeowners in Brooklyn and Queens. But the claim wasn't that the bank was "redlining," refusing to lend money to minority borrowers. Just the opposite. The article alleged that the lender had pushed African-American borrowers into taking out high-cost home-equity loans that they did not need and could not afford. The problem—according to *The Times* at least—wasn't too *little* credit, it was too *much*. It was Martin Luther King Day, as I remember, and I ripped the story out of the paper, handed it to my civil rights chief (we were on the way to a church in Harlem for an MLK celebration), and we agreed we had to get to the bottom of this new issue.

Andy Celli, who was the chief of the civil rights bureau, was one of those lawyers with whom you just wanted to be a partner. A spectacular writer and thoughtful in the extreme, he understood the role that the law could and should play in transforming our society. It was not just a set of antiseptic rules, it was a vehicle with purpose. In fact, Andy was the first colleague I persuaded to join the AG's office after I was elected, and I have been eternally thankful for that decision—his and mine.

Andy then did one of the many things he did spectacularly well—he began to investigate a story that threw our instinct on its head: Instead of lending too little, were banks actually lending too much? And if so, how could that make sense?

Andy started by interviewing the homeowners profiled in the *Times* article, and the advocacy group that was organizing around "the problem." Of course, that was only the first step. He sought input from community and faith leaders about what they were seeing, and he gathered statistical data from think tanks and government sources. HMDA—a federal statute—requires the collection and reporting of home mortgage lending information by race and neighborhood of the borrowers. This data was vitally important. We researched the laws, studying how Congress and the state Legislature regulate the mortgage market, and what remedies might be available for violations. And of course, he reached out to the lender and its associated businesses—the bankers, agents, brokers, and other financial professionals who marketed, sold, papered, and closed these home loans in the field—for their perspective. "Reached out" is really just a nice way of saying *subpoenaed*.

There's nothing quite like a subpoena to get a company's attention. The subpoena asked for copies of all of the loan-related documents generated over the previous three years.[1]

The documents, as it turned out, were the key to the whole thing. (This was a lesson that would be learned in every financial case we made—on Wall Street or Main Street. The hard work of reading all the paper was the key to success.)

There were tens of thousands of pages of documents, reflecting loans to thousands of individual homeowners in New York City. On the surface, these documents had all the earmarks of the free market's efficiently distributing credit to customers in need. The records were in perfect order: signed and countersigned loan documents, disclosure forms duly initialed by the borrower, and underwriting score sheets that seemed to bear the imprint of sober consideration before the "Approved" stamp was applied. Just what you'd expect to find in the files of a legitimate mortgage bank.

Clearly, the lender had "checked all right boxes." But did the loans actually make sense—economic sense—for both the lender *and* the borrowers? That was the big question. As we've learned from long experience, it isn't hard to create the *impression* of fairness in any transaction—that's what "fine print" is all about. But to really understand whether the market is operating cleanly as well as smoothly, you have to ask the question: Would any reasonable consumer take this deal if they actually understood what the economic impact was going to be?

The mortgage loans we reviewed that spring of 1999 flunked this test miserably—every last one of them did, for a number of different reasons. Start with the interest rate—the "price" of the loans to the consumers. In those days, the prevailing interest rate for ordinary borrowers was somewhere around 7 percent. Yet these loans bore interests rates of 12 percent, 13 percent, even 14 percent. Now, high prices aren't necessarily an indication of illegality of course. After all, sometimes market conditions dictate high prices, for perfectly legitimate reasons. This is precisely what the lender's lawyers argued to us. They suggested that the elevated interest rates—up to twice the prime rate—were justified because the people who were borrowing money had "poor credit histories." It was what we might call the "free market defense": We charge more for our loans to account for the risk that the borrowers will never pay them back. "Subprime lending," they called it. It was the first time I'd heard the term—but it wouldn't be the last.

As I have said repeatedly, I believe in the market: one that functions according to the rules and laws of economics. Where market conditions—credit risk, competition, etc.—justify higher interest rates, I not only have no problem with that, it is precisely the way the system is supposed to work. In such circumstances, government must stay its hand.

But as we dug into the records, we found that the facts of *this* case were otherwise. Specifically, in loan after loan after high-cost loan, we found three things that startled us, three things that proved that the "free market defense" was, in essence, thoroughly flawed.

First, we found a consistent pattern of the mortgage lender's selling loans to people *without regard to their ability to repay.* Let me say that again: This was a mortgage lender who didn't seem to care if a borrower had enough income to make the payment on the loan, and often didn't even check. In a world where credit is hard to come by and banks are tight-fisted, this is difficult to imagine. But 1999 was the leading edge of the credit bubble. And this particular bank was simply eager to make the loans—at the elevated interest rates we discussed earlier—and get the borrower scrambling to make the monthly obligations. And make the payments people did, at least briefly, for fear of losing their homes. In some cases, homeowners went without basic necessities just to pay back these high interest loans.

Isn't it just too risky for a mortgage lender to make a loan without caring whether the person borrowing the money could pay it back? The answer is simple: For these loans, there was little if any risk at all to the lender.

That's because as soon as any particular mortgage loan transaction was completed with the borrower, and the lender had received its fees from the deal, the lender *re-sold* the loan to Wall Street, as part of a package or "tranche" of loans. Securitization of this debt was the new game in town. Each loan would be bundled with others, and the risk that any one loan wouldn't be repaid was spread out across the broader market. This was the opening moment when Wall Street grew enamored of the mythology that alchemy could be applied to bad debt. Enough of it bundled together could turn lead into gold. It was a perfect scheme. With the credit risk passed along, re-sold again and again, and shuttled around Wall Street, the original lender ended up bearing almost *no* risk at all. It was precisely this pass-the-buck practice that led to the mortgage crisis of 2008. But when we first started looking at subprime mortgage lending practices in 1999, the crisis was very much in the future.

The second remarkable thing we found was that, in some cases, the very people who were offered loans at up to 14 percent actually had *good* credit histories, and could qualify for much less expensive loans—even loans at the then-prime rate of 7 percent. Whereas the lender claimed that these borrowers were deadbeats (or were at risk of becoming deadbeats), that just was not true. What we found instead were working-class Americans—teachers and post office workers, clerical workers and (many) retirees—who pinched their pennies and faithfully paid their bills every month and who were being sold debt at much *higher* interest costs than they should have borne. And this was because the brokers who were supposed to be looking out for the borrower were given incentives to push up the rate on the loans. This was contrary to law.

And finally, we found extensive evidence of the practice known as "flipping," when a lender, often working with a broker, pressures a homeowner to refinance an existing mortgage loan for a new one *with more onerous terms*. From a purely economic perspective, "flipped" loans make no sense at all. Far from improving the circumstance of the borrower, they do nothing more than generate fees and higher rates for the lender and its brokers. It's selling a consumer something she didn't need, and overcharging her in the process.

In the home-equity lending environment that prevailed in Brooklyn and Queens in the late 1990s, everything was upside down. Brokers who played the seemingly benign role of connecting would-be borrowers with banks willing to lend got paid extra commissions—kickbacks, really—if they sold the borrower a more expensive, higher-interest loan. And "fees" generally described as merely covering the costs of pulling the paperwork together sometimes accounted for upwards of 10 per-cent of the overall loan—a huge profit center for the lender. The laws of rational economic behavior, where prices were negotiated, middle-man helped forge compromise, and lenders were limited in what they could change by competitive pressure and cold, hard economic facts, had been suspended. The free market, in short, had failed. And in the process a genuine monster was being created: The magnitude of bad debt that was soon coursing through the pipeline of Wall Street would metastasize into the bubble and collapse of 2008. Yet nobody wanted to admit this. The profits were simply too big.

And there was one more thing—one more, ugly, unmistakable, unde-niable thing about this whole mess: These wildly overpriced, economi-cally irrational loans were overwhelmingly sold to African-American and Latino homeowners, living in predominantly minority neighbor-hoods. When you looked at it on a map, it took your breath away. Vir-tually every loan of this type was made within census tracts with more than 80 percent minority residents. Where the "whiter" neighborhoods abutted those census tracts, the lending stopped—right at the border. This was true even where the adjacent white neighborhood bore the same economic characteristics—poverty rates, foreclosure rates, etc.—as the targeted minority neighborhoods. This wasn't "redlining" in the classic sense. It was the reverse: using African-American and Latino neighborhoods as a target for the very worst credit products on the mar-ket. And it was no coincidence.

So, after five months of interviewing witnesses, reviewing documents, researching the law, and discussing our findings with the top people in the office, we reached a conclusion. The free market had failed—or, more correctly, it had been perverted by a bad actor and perverse incen-tives. Worse yet, there was an ugly racial tinge to the whole thing. Rather than immediately file a lawsuit for a raft of legal violations, we did what we would almost always do: try to negotiate a resolution that would re-solve the market failure in a way that comported with what should be the rules of the market.

It was my view then, and my view now, that, except in the most ex-treme cases, the blunt instrument of a government lawsuit should be a last resort, and that fair, effective and market-friendly resolutions are of-ten best reached by consent of the parties without the filing of a lawsuit. And so, as I would do more often than I could count over the next eight years as AG, I directed my team to call in the target company's executives and legal team and explain to them our theory of their wrongdoing. For all the criticism we would later get for being "too tough" on companies in trouble, we never hid the ball from them. In virtually every case, before we brought the hammer down, we showed them our cards, and offered them some form of a negotiated settlement.

In this case, the basic thrust of the settlement I offered—and that the lender ultimately accepted—was to require that the company be true to free market principles. Here, the request was simple: Going forward, the loans made would have to make economic sense, for both the borrower and the lender, and that, looking backward, borrowers who had been victimized would get some relief from the toxic, illegal loans they'd been sold. In practice, we were pretty specific about what that meant. We required that the lender consider the borrowers' ability to repay the loan before making it, rather than simply relying upon the fact that it could get its money out quickly by reselling the loan and/or foreclosing on it if things went bad. We required that the interest rates and fees charged be consistent with market conditions—not just a reflection of what the lender could get away with. We banned "flipping"—the practice of leaving a borrower worse off with a new loan than she would be if she hadn't borrowed at all. And we outlawed pointless and exorbitant "fees," which were pure price-gouging and never justified by any economic measure.

Looking at the thousands of borrowers who were stuck with these awful loans and were already in foreclosure, we asked, and the lender agreed, to cease eviction proceedings for a while, and to set aside $6 million to reform some of the worst loans. It was not a small sum, given the volume of loans the company had made. Finally, we insisted upon a court-appointed monitor—a neutral third party—who would watch over the lender's practices for three years to ensure that it was fully complying with the terms it had agreed to.

None of the things that we asked for, and none of the things that the lender agreed to do, violated the basic principles of a genuine market. Indeed, they actually enforced and supported these very principles. But it took a governmental actor—with its investigatory powers, its resources, its will, and frankly its leverage—to give life to those principles. The market had failed—or, more correctly, been undermined by a bad actor. Our job was to right that balance.

But still that left the question: Why exactly did this happen? Had "one bad apple"[2] gotten away with upending the iron laws of "free market" capitalism? After all, if one bad lender is overpricing its products and taking advantage of its customers, why wouldn't a "good lender" swoop in, offer consumers better deals, and steal away all the business? That is the argument of those who are opposed to government intervention. That hadn't happened, of course, and I wondered why. I had a theory, albeit one based only on a series of educated guesses, not hard evidence.

My theory was that the so-called "good" banks—the *national* banks, who sponsor sports stadiums and tennis matches—were not doing much better by their minority customers than renegades like the one we had investigated. If they had been, I figured, the lender we ended up prosecuting would've been punished not by government, but by its competitors and the market itself.

I wondered for years, on and off, whether there was any evidence to support this theory. I had the hope that our settlement with the one lender would cause other banks to adopt best practices, and that credit would flow more freely in poor, predominately minority neighborhoods. But by 2005, I looked around at the home mortgage market and I got the sinking feeling that the change we had hoped for and worked hard to achieve with one lender did not seem to have penetrated the big, national banks. In fact, by 2005, "subprime lending" had become the darling of Wall Street—and I had the nagging sense (and more than a few live complaints) that communities of color were being targeted, again, for the very worst loans. So, I sent some letters out—just letters, not subpoenas—asking the nation's largest banks to provide my office with some basic information. I wanted to know how many loans these banks had made to minority homeowners, why the interest rates on those loans tended to be higher than loans to white borrowers, and what market conditions—risk factors, creditworthiness measures, etc.— the banks had used to set their prices. Given what I had already seen, and sought to address in New York, it seemed like a reasonable enough request.

Something was clearly amiss in the mortgage markets—and we wanted to get a better fix on what it was. We didn't know yet that the tsunami of bad debt that crashed the economy was forming, but we knew something was going on that merited asking a few questions.

Judging from the reaction, you would have thought I'd announced my intention to implement *The Communist Manifesto* by force of arms. And, incredibly, it wasn't only the national banks who were howling and filing a lawsuit against me—although howl, and sue, they did. The Bush Administration itself, through its Office of the Comptroller of the Currency (OCC), sued me too, winning a court order directing that I stop asking questions! It had to be one of the most ironic lawsuits in the history of American jurisprudence. The Bush Administration claimed that my office lacked the legal authority to ask such impertinent questions, because the federal OCC was the only government agency empowered to do so. Yet, as we knew even then, and would see even more clearly in the years that followed, the OCC and other federal agencies charged with overseeing the financial services industry seemed congenitally incapable of asking *any* questions of Wall Street—much less the hard ones that we wanted answers to.

Typical of the conservative reaction to our inquiry was a *National Review* cover story ticking off the cases we had made, labeling me the "litigation devil" and the "most destructive politician in America"—see the cover caricature of me below—because we had actually thought to

investigate subprime lending! As the article said: "Until the Treasury Department told him to back off, Spitzer was contemplating action against subprime mortgage lenders, whose predation has 'become a new scourge' to quote an article he co-wrote in *The New Republic*." Looking back, we look somewhat prescient, and the *National Review*'s typical misunderstanding of the role government needs to play looks somewhat predictable.

Well, if that isn't enough irony for one case, you need to hear how it all ended up. As I mentioned, the Bush Administration won its injunction against our office in the trial court, and in an appellate court. There was only one more court to appeal to: the U.S. Supreme Court. To my amazement, the Supreme Court took the case, and ruled in our favor. Justice Antonin Scalia, the Court's leading conservative, wrote the opinion of the Court, with the four more liberal justices joining him to make a majority. While the reasoning that Justice Scalia offered centered on the role of courts in interpreting agency rules, as dry a legal topic as there ever was, I came to believe that Justice Scalia's real motive for going our way was his respect for states' rights. After all, the right and duty of states to innovate in particular areas—to serve, as Justice Brandeis once said, as "little laboratories" of regulatory experimentation—is a conservative notion, not a liberal one. I think that's what appealed to Scalia.

Whatever the motivation, the victory was sweet. But what stays with me even today is what I honestly believe to have been behind the Bush Administration's lawsuit in the first place: the fear they and the banks had that we were about to upend the enormously profitable pipeline of subprime mortgage lending that was driving so much of their business. Even though we merely wanted to ensure sound business and lending practices and ensure that no discrimination was ongoing, the banks and the OCC were horrified at the prospect of our inquiry.

And so, despite our efforts to dig into what was the largest negative externality in our economy, one that would cause the metastasizing effect that ultimately brought the economy down in 2008, the agency that had the single greatest obligation to enforce and understand the dangers being created by massive bad debt coursing into the economy sided with the banks, not with either consumers or the market principles it should have been there to protect.

While the particular remedy might vary from case to case and sector to sector, the imperative to examine the marketplace carefully and to recognize that market failures can cause externalities that distort the level and type of production is critical. Private parties acting alone can produce a result that is not socially optimal. Too much pollution in the air and too much debt in the securitization pipeline are just two examples of this. In such cases, even the most conservative economists would have to acknowledge that some form of intervention is needed to remedy the problem. Failure to do so can let market failures overwhelm the economy: From global warming to debt-driven bubbles and crashes, the failure to understand these negative externalities can be harsh and dangerous. If the so-called "free market" voices who opposed all our efforts in these domains had not been able to squelch real inquiries, we might have been able to avoid the serious consequences of market failures.

3

SELF-REGULATION

Rule Three:

Markets can't regulate themselves,

and companies can't

police their own bad behavior.

At the core of the market-based ideology that swept our nation, beginning with President Reagan and culminating in the crash of 2008, was a clear belief—propagated by the leading voices in business, academia, conservative politicians, and even some of the most prominent members of the judiciary—that the regulatory and enforcement structure of government simply wasn't necessary. Business leaders themselves could set standards of behavior that would ensure ethical conduct and fairness to consumers and the marketplace. A veritable alphabet soup of industry organizations was created, in every sector from Wall Street to pharmaceuticals to food, designed to send the same message: Trust Us! We will police ourselves.

Yet the notion that business can or would do so is one of the great myths that sowed the seeds of our economic cataclysm. We can't and wouldn't let football players call their own holding penalties, or have a batter call balls and strikes. Similarly, the notion that a market can thrive and that principles of integrity, fairness, and fiduciary duty can survive in the dog-eat-dog world of the market without serious enforcement is simply naïve, or worse, an intentional deception by those who wish to benefit from a lack of enforcement.

Still, once politicians embraced the argument that enforcement was an unnecessary burden, and that issues relating to enforcement were better left to industry itself, we denied the structure of enforcement the intellectual energy and integrity it needed to do its job. Every enforcement effort was assaulted as an attack on markets, rather than being the necessary protection and definition of the market. The agencies charged with ensuring that markets could work were cast as the enemy of markets. We headed down a path that both starved the enforcement agencies of the funding they needed to do their jobs and, much more importantly, sapped them of the creativity, energy, and dedication needed to stand up to powerful forces that could override their efforts. Enforcement agencies were denigrated as "mere" government bureaucrats, low-level functionaries, whose very role in life was contrary to all we believed in. Enforcement agencies and those who spoke on their behalf were the orphans of Washington society: ignored, derided, outcasts. And an entire intellectual facade for this Potemkin village was created—often by academics who were being paid by the very companies who benefited from the argument itself.

The underlying intellectual deception of the self-regulatory doctrine, and its dangers, were driven home to me in the midst of the so-called "analyst" cases—the first of the mega Wall Street cases that we brought. Although I will describe the entire case in more detail later, this one vignette is worth recounting right at the top:

We had uncovered one of the most massive securities market deceptions imaginable: Merrill Lynch, one of the largest retail brokerage houses, was recommending that consumers buy stocks even though analysts at Merrill knew the stocks would be bad investments. The reason was simple: Merrill was being paid by the companies whose stocks they were recommending.

But horrific as all this was—and it led to what was at the time perhaps the most important series of settlements and restructurings that Wall Street had seen in many years—the bizarrely revealing statements of the lawyers for Merrill were even more troubling.

As we had gathered our evidence, and as the magnitude of the deceptions and ingrained structural nature of the fraud was becoming clear to me, I had a series of conversations with counsel for Merrill. As it became clear that a settlement would not be possible before we actually brought our case, one of the lawyers for Merrill had a poignant argument: Eliot, he said, "Be careful. We have powerful friends." That is a direct quotation.

I had not, as Attorney General, or anywhere else for that matter, been the object of such a brazen threat or assertion of raw power. But the lawyer was right: They did have powerful friends, and this fact had helped Merrill and others stave off all sorts of prosecutions in the past. But the fact that this genuinely wise lawyer would roll this out as an argument that he believed might dissuade me from bringing the case, quite frankly, stupefied me. My response was not printable, and we filed the case the next business day.

But it got worse. Shortly after we filed the case, the attorneys from Merrill came down to my office. Usually attorneys representing a major company in this context make a series of arguments: You don't understand the business; you took the emails out of context; the behavior was simply that of a rogue employee; there is more subtlety here than you want to acknowledge. These are the often specious arguments made by sophisticated white-collar defense counsel—usually in that order. Of course, they can also be true on occasion.

But the lawyers from Merrill, some of the finest lawyers in NYC, didn't make any of those arguments. They looked at me and they said: "Eliot, you are right about what Merrill has done. But we are not as bad as our competitors. Everybody does it, and everybody knows it."

I was stunned. This was as straightforward and complete an admission as I had ever heard from a corporation—surely this early in a case. Yet it laid bare something much deeper: The entire facade of self-regulation, the alleged capacity of the most powerful securities companies in the world to exercise the self-restraint not to commit ongoing fraud, was simply that—a facade. It was just one more smoke screen, one more layer of the underlying deception. Not only was Merrill actually committing the very offenses we alleged—and indeed the CEO of Merrill publicly apologized just a few days later—but the lawyers were acknowledging that the entire industry was aware, and had done nothing.[3]

Why? Simple: Because, in the absence of outside enforcement, the behavior of the lowest common denominator would dictate moral behavior for the entire marketplace. As one company and then another sank lower and lower, misleading the public and stock investors, and gaining by doing so, and without any enforcement actions being taken, every other company followed suit. None of the companies was willing to sacrifice market share in the lucrative investment banking sector in order to restore integrity to the analytical work they were providing to their customers. Not once did the companies, individually or together, act to raise the bar or intervene to stop clearly fraudulent behavior. There was not a single bit of noise or meaningful action from any of the self-regulatory bodies.

And to make it even worse, all the government agencies—from the SEC to the DOJ and other regulatory bodies—that were charged with stopping this type of behavior had done nothing. They, too, sat quietly by, watching as the public was deceived by the so-called "advice" being given.

The statements of the lawyers made clear that any pretense that the companies could regulate themselves was long gone. The companies all understood the way the market was functioning: they all knew there was a major problem, but they did nothing; they—but not the public— all benefited. That was the way it was, the way it had been, and the way it would continue to be if they were left to their own devices.

If their first line of defense was "we all do it," their second, astonishingly, was "everybody knows." In essence they were saying, "everybody knows we are lying, so the lies are harmless"! The banks wanted us to believe that since those on the inside were clever enough to know that the analyst recommendations to buy or sell were a result of conflicted thinking, and shouldn't be relied upon, everybody else must know that as well. Therefore, since nobody could reasonably rely on the recommendations being made, nobody was harmed. No harm no foul—as we say on the ball field.

The problem, of course, is that the "everybody knows" defense is not sustainable. The investment banks had spent gobs of money marketing the value of their stock recommendations as a way or promoting their retail brokerage organizations. And unfortunately, many people, to their detriment, had relied upon the recommendations made by the banks. To suddenly disparage the value of these recommendations and claim that everybody knew them to be worthless was at best duplicitous.

But the most fundamental point was this: Self-regulation is—and was—an oxymoron. The banks were simultaneously admitting that everybody in the industry knew about the underlying conflicts that generated unreliable and often outright false stock recommendations, and also that neither they nor anybody else in the industry had done anything about it. The notion that we could rely upon the industry to regulate itself was gone. The entire facade that had been erected by the business world was nothing but a mirage.

And to this day, I have yet to get a satisfactory answer to this simple question: Name one major scandal where an industry has brought to the government's attention a significant fraud that was generating profits for an industry or company.

So let's dig a bit deeper into what Merrill and all the other major investment houses were doing, and how their supposedly diligent and careful self-regulatory framework had not only failed to do anything about the massive structural fraud being perpetrated on the public, but how the pretense of self-regulation was aided and abetted by covering up the fraud.

A bit of backdrop: A major investment bank like Merrill Lynch had many different silos. Two of the most important are the traditional investment banking role, or "IB" role, of issuing and marketing stocks of new companies—initial public offerings—and, in a supposedly separate silo, the analytical function of recommending stocks to be bought and sold by the investing public. The IPO part of the business was—and is—enormously profitable. The fees generated are vast, and so being selected to do IPOs for companies is essential to the success of the entire company. The second silo is filled by analysts who are supposed to provide independent and objective recommendations to Merrill retail clients. Maintaining this independence is, of course, essential to the integrity of the recommendations being given to the investing public.

Merrill, however, in complete disregard of the importance of maintaining this divide, essentially made the analysts part of the Investment Banking division, having them participate in the effort to get IB clients by promising IB clients affirmative coverage of the stocks, and by making the analysts' compensation dependent upon how successful they were in getting companies to use Merrill for their IB IPO work.

Our investigation—based on the review of over 30,000 documents; over 100,000 pages, many of them emails; and interviews of over 20 witnesses under oath and countless more not under oath—established beyond any doubt that the effect was to subvert the integrity of the Merrill stock rating system. In the Internet sector, a hot area for IPO activity during this period, not a single "reduce" or "sell" recommendation was given during the time frame we examined—primarily, we alleged, because the analysts were effectively just marketers for the investment banking arm of the bank. Investors were told to buy or hold every stock that Merrill rated, even as some of those stocks plummeted in value to near zero.

Merrill, of course, maintained in all its marketing materials that it was purely objective in its analysis. According to an affidavit in the case, the company told the public: "Opinions expressed by Analysts must be objective. Any indication that a Research opinion is less than totally objective, or that it may have been influenced by a business relationship of the Firm, could seriously damage the Firm's reputation and lead to potential legal liability."

Of course, the conflicts that led to not a single "reduce" or "sell" rating's being issued by the Internet group were rife. Indeed, in a moment of honesty, Henry Blodgett, one of Merrill's superstar analysts, had threatened to "start calling the stocks... like we see them, no matter what the ancillary business consequences are," the affidavit says.

Instead of ever alerting the public to the fact that a stock was ripe for a price decline, Merrill would simply drop coverage altogether. The investors who relied upon Merrill's analysts would never know that the stock was one they should sell.

To understand the deception being perpetrated, you need to understand the 1 to 5 numerical system Merrill used to grade stocks:

1. Buy (20% or more price growth expected)
2. Accumulate (10% to 20% price growth expected)
3. Neutral (10% price growth to 10% price drop expected of price)
4. Reduce (10% to 20% price drop expected)
5. Sell (20% or more price drop expected)

The ratings were issued with two numbers—the first relating to the intermediate term, or through the next 12 months, and the second number relating to the longer term, beyond 12 months.

With that in mind, consider this excerpt from the affidavit:

> "[O]n August 30, 1999, the group initiated coverage on the stock
> of Internet Capital Group (ICGE), an investment banking client,
> with a 2–1 rating. The stock closed on October 4, 2000 at $15.69,
> down from a high of $212 on December 22, 1999. On October 5,
> 2000 with the stock at $12.38, in an e-mail exchange with another
> senior analyst, Blodget predicted the stock was, "going to 5." (ML
> 63900). The next day he wrote in an e-mail: "No helpful news to
> relate [regarding ICGE], I'm afraid. This has been a disaster... there
> really is no floor to the stock."(ML 63901). But even with these prog-
> nostications, the public rating remained 2–1 and, when eventually
> downgraded on November 9, 2000, was changed only to a 2–2. The
> result was a continued recommendation to the investing public to
> purchase a stock about which the head of the Internet group was
> obviously exceptionally and accurately pessimistic, and for which
> he anticipated a drop of an additional 60 percent. (ML 63900–01;
> ML 64077; ML 53507). Despite this pessimistic outlook, ICGE was
> on Merrill Lynch's list of the top ten technology stocks ("Top Ten
> Tech" list), as late as September 12, 2000."

The following chart, which was in our initial court filing, gives a few
other examples of the stark divergence between the true beliefs of the
analysts and their publicly stated recommendation:

COMPANY	DATE	CONTEMPORANEOUS ANALYST COMMENTS	PUB-LISHED RATING
Aether Systems (AETH)	03/15/01	"might have announcement next week... which could pop stock... but fundamentals horrible" (ML82578)	3–1
Excite@home (ATHM)	12/27/99 12/29/99	"we are neutral on the stock" Six month outlook is "flat", without any "real catalysts" for improvement seen (ML 37899; ML37956)	2–1
Excite@home (ATHM)	06/03/00	"such a piece of crap" (ML51453)	2–1
GoTo.Com (GOTO)	1/11/01	Nothing interesting about company "except banking fees" (ML03806)	3–1
InfoSpace (INSP)	7/13/00	"this stock is a powder keg, given how aggressive we were on it earlier this year and given the 'bad smell' comments that so many institutions are bringing up" (ML06413)	1–1
InfoSpace (INSP)	10/20/00	"piece of junk" (ML06578)	1–1

Internet Capital Group Inc. (ICGE)	10/05/00	"Going to 5» (closed at $12.38) (ML63901)	2-1
Internet Capital Group Inc. (ICGE)	10/06/00	"No hopeful news to relate.... We see nothing that will turn this around near-term. The company needs to restructure its operations and raise additional cash, and until it does that, there is nothing positive to say." (ML64077)	2-1
Lifeminders (LFMN)	12/04/00	"POS" (piece of shit) (ML60903)	2-1
24/7 Media (TFSM)	10/10/00	"piece of shit" (ML64372)	2-2

Every element of the research that Merrill analysts provided to the public was influenced by the reality that appeasing the investment bankers was central to the research function—even though it fundamentally degraded the integrity of research. As the affidavit quoted one researcher as saying, "part of the reason we didn't highlight [a risk] is because we wanted to protect ICG's banking business." Another was quoted as saying, "the whole idea that we are independent of banking is a big lie." Management itself acknowledged that "we are off base on how we rate stocks and how much we bend over backwards to accommodate banking," according to the affidavit.

The affidavit submitted by Eric DiNallo, the head of my office's Investor Protection division, was a bombshell—thoroughly destroying the carefully crafted and false notion that Wall Street research could or should be relied upon by the investing public.

The irony is that in the weeks leading up to the filing of the case we had been having settlement talks that ended up foundering on one simple issue: Merrill's demand that we seal the emails that were so damning. I was firmly convinced that much of the value of the case was to reveal to the public what was going on inside Wall Street, and to seal the emails would defeat that very purpose. So I refused.

I also explained to Merrill's attorneys that their choice was simple: Either the emails would be released as part of a settlement, or they would be revealed in an accusatory instrument in a much harsher light. Why they didn't settle and have the release of the emails tempered by the fact of a settlement is still mystifying to me. Perhaps they didn't take seriously my very clear statements about our preparedness to file a complaint that would set out for all to see the magnitude of their violation of the public trust. And maybe they didn't quite realize that telling me they "had powerful friends" was not exactly a way to negotiate effectively with me.

In some ways this was the first major case that highlighted the power of emails to provide insight into the contemporaneous thinking of the author. In fact, the focus on emails led to this humorous ad in *The Wall Street Journal*:

Mere days after we filed our case, the CEO of Merrill issued an extraordinary apology, and shortly thereafter we entered a preliminary settlement with Merrill, which obligated them to sever the links between compensation for analysts and investment banking, ensure that there was in fact a separation between the analytical and investment banking parts of their bank, create a slew of other review procedures and disclosures that would better ensure integrity in their work, issue a public apology for their failure of integrity, and pay $100 million. But this was a mere prelude to the so-called "global deal" we would negotiate in the coming months.

All of this led up to what was perhaps one of the more intriguing evenings I got to spend as Attorney General. Even as we were still investigating many of the major banks and the quality of their analytical work, I received an invitation to speak at the Institutional Investor Annual awards dinner for Wall Street analysts. At first I thought it was a joke. Why would they possibly invite me? This was the annual gathering of Wall Street analysts, and, as one might imagine, I was not a terribly popular figure in that crowd. When I went, and was approaching the dais to deliver my remarks, it was one of the few times I actually felt I needed security.

But when I got to the podium, I decided to do one better than merely inform the analysts of their less-than-spectacular results and the conflicted nature of the business model they relied upon. Since we had been investigating many of the very people in the audience, and parsing their derogatory internal commentary about the very stocks they were at the same time recommending to the public, I opened by saying: "It is nice to put faces to the emails!" The crowd howled with a combination of anguish, humor, and venom.

In the course of the first week after filing our case, in chatting with Eric DiNallo and the others on the team, I said I was sure that the Securities and Exchange Commission would jump in and take over the case immediately. To my amazement, they didn't. They were uniquely timorous during this stretch of time—hesitant to even recognize that there were structural issues that needed to be confronted: They were stuck in an out-of-date rut in terms of how cases should be resolved and prosecuted. They still believed in the false notion of self-regulation; this was, in fact, Harvey Pitt's SEC—a "kinder, gentler SEC." Unfortunately for the public, it seemed to me that Pitt had internalized the defenses he had made on behalf of his clients when he was a defense attorney. There was no way he would bring the requisite aggressiveness to his job as chairman of the SEC.

A very brief detour: For years the SEC has claimed that its inability to ferret out Wall Street wrongdoing was a consequence of underfunding. Nothing could be further from the truth. If anything, they have too much money and have as a consequence grown complacent and thoughtless in how they spend it. They have demonstrated a lack of creativity and analytical skill in failing to ask where improper market structures and dynamics were generating significant frauds that affected the public. They have grown grotesquely bureaucratic and failed to react either to leads that were generated by whistleblowers or to clear signals that something was awry in the capital markets.

What emerged over the course of our investigation was a clear understanding of the improper three-party transaction that had guided so much of what went on. First, analysts misled the public by putting "buy" ratings on virtually every stock, helping the investment bankers persuade the companies to hire the investment bank—the promise of a "buy" rating on the stock was the bait for the companies to hire either Merrill—or any other investment bank. For this the analysts were compensated with huge bonuses, part of the fees paid by the client companies to the investment banks. Second, the investment bankers made huge fees on the deals—running the IPO's was a huge money maker for the investment banks. The third corner of the deal was that the CEOs of the companies who were clients of the investment banks were allocated shares of the "hot stocks" in IPOs, cutting them into the instant cash that was made when these stocks went public. Being allocated a piece of a hot IPO was candy to the CEOs, who received the shares individually—often to the tune of tens of millions of dollars.

So the analysts, investment bankers, and CEOs all won. The losers? Regular investors who relied on the analysts for advice.

In a subsequent series of cases, we sued a number of CEOs alleging, and winning, on the theory that the cash they made on these hot stock allocations should have gone to the shareholders of the companies they worked for. The CEOs were being given the shares as an inducement to bring their business to that particular investment bank—and so this was no different conceptually from any commercial bribe paid to an employee to direct business to one vendor or another. In fact, in the final "global deal" we negotiated, we put in place a total ban on this practice, which had come to be known as "spinning."

The global deal we executed with the ten major investment banks formalized the divide between the analytical work the banks issued to the public and their retail clients, and the investment banking work they did. It required all sorts of disclosures on the part of the banks, imposed a fine of $1.4 billion, and perhaps, most creatively, required that the banks provide their clients with independent research—from analysts who worked for outfits with no conflicts whatsoever. This was an effort to do what we had done with the Gambinos and trucking: restructure the industry to remedy the underlying problem.

The analyst case was a story of conflicts of interest, violations of fiduciary duty, and the failure of the single most central piece of the false dogma that got us to the precipice in 2008: that self-regulation can be relied upon to stave off fraud and improprieties. Not once did any of the major investment banks, individually or collectively, take any action to forestall the continued degradation of research.

This entire mentality was summed up by two great statements, one by Jack Grubman, a famed telecom analyst, the other by Chuck Prince, the CEO of Citibank who succeeded Sandy Weill. Grubman said that "what once was a conflict of interest is now viewed as a synergy." What a marvelous way to delude oneself into not recognizing the fundamental impropriety of what one was doing. The conflicts were there, obvious, and the only "synergies" were for those who were making money on both sides of the transactions—the investment bankers and analysts. Investors were, to say it politely, getting the short end of the stick.

Of the business practices during the run-up to the bubble, Prince observed: "As long as the music is playing, you've got to get up to dance. We're still dancing." Nobody at the banks—no matter how smart they claim to be—ever thought that maybe it was time to stop feeding quarters into the jukebox that was playing the music. So much for self-regulation. And dance they did, until we all paid the price.

HIDING THE DIRT:

HOW BIG PHARMA TRIED TO

OVERSELL AND KEEP

THE UGLY STUFF QUIET

The failure of self-regulation manifested itself in other sectors as well, of course. Imagine if you were selling a drug and had created a nice marketing argument that the drug was good for teenagers as an antidepressant. But also imagine that your studies showed that every now and then after a teenager took the drug he was going to be tempted to commit suicide. Well, you might be tempted to keep that last little fact away from the public. It sure wouldn't help sell the drug. And folks finding out that a consequence of taking a drug is perhaps having kids become suicidal might think once or twice about subsidizing or paying for the drug with government money. This was the focus of our case involving Glaxo and Paxil.

While a failure of self-regulation can often lead to harm, this case was so much more fundamental. It affected the health of kids and highlighted the depths to which big pharma would go to grab profits and market share, without regard to the underlying well-being of patients.

The entire saga of this story is beautifully told in a remarkable and reasonably brief book, *Side Effects*, written by Alison Bass. I will not try to reiterate the entirety of the story. But the critical point to establish is that when a market functions without full disclosure of information, when conflicts of interest are hidden, and when as a consequence consumers are misled, dangerous things can happen. The greed of one company here totally overran any sense of ethical obligation. The notion that we could rely upon big pharma to regulate itself, to apply any constraints on its own behavior, was totally destroyed by this case. Once again, the myth of reliance on self-regulation had generated the potential for enormous harm.

The remarkable and tenacious work of several lawyers in the AG's office—Rose Firestein, Tom Conway, and Joe Baker in particular—brought to light a simple and devastating fact: GlaxoSmithKline, the manufacturer of the much prescribed drug Paxil, had fundamentally misrepresented the lack of efficacy of the drug and had also hidden the significant data that indicated that teenagers in particular who used the drug might be susceptible to suicidal tendencies. At first it was hard to believe this might be the case. The so-called "peer-reviewed" journal articles about the drug both indicated that it worked as an anti-depressant, and that there were no significant side effects. Neither statement was correct.

When Rose began to dig into the underlying truths of the situation, she discovered that not only were the articles wrong, but that the company had been able, with impunity, to refuse to reveal the actual data, keeping from the marketplace the facts necessary to determine whether the drug was being wisely prescribed. Only because Rose was able to get her hands on some of the underlying testing data was she able to determine that the public representations being made by the company were flat out false—and were directly contrary to their own testing data. And indeed, that the company had suppressed four of its own studies refuting the claims it made in public.

The sole major study on Paxil's effectiveness, in *The Journal of American Academy of Child and Adolescent Psychiatry*, stated conclusions that were directly belied by the underlying data. And yet nobody at the company had stepped forward to cry foul, to object in any significant way, or to make clear the fundamental distortion. And nobody outside the company could do so, because they couldn't get their hands on the data.

The entire world of pharmaceutical trials, the clinical testing data that was at the heart of medical determinations, was one that permitted positive tests to be published—those that supported the claims of the company—and negative tests to be suppressed. There was virtually no accountability.

We demanded as a remedy that Glaxo publish the actual testing data, so that there could be an honest and open evaluation of the merits of the drug. But here was the key: The remedy we sought was not just limited to this one drug: we required that Glaxo alter the methodology of publishing *ALL* clinical testing trials. Glaxo was required to establish an online "Clinical Trials Registry" that would contain summaries of results for all GSK-sponsored clinical studies of drugs conducted after December 27, 2000. The Registry had to encompass summaries of the results of clinical studies in a standardized format, for over 20 categories of information, including those regarding the effectiveness of the drug tested, the type and severity of adverse side effects the study participants experienced, whether the goals or other components of the study were changed midstream, and whether the study was terminated early before full completion—and if so, why.

The importance of this was reiterated by the president of the New York State Psychiatric Association, who said "The settlement will insure that clinical drug research by GSK for all drugs will be available in a publicly accessible data base.... We hope that this settlement establishes a precedent for the pharmaceutical industry and for all clinical researchers."

Our hope was that this information would permit informed judgments to be made by the doctors who actually prescribed the medicines, and would go a long way toward preventing the biased pieces that had too often been published in respected medical journals touting drugs, when the actual data revealed something altogether different.

The database has had significant and important consequences. Just one example: On August 12, 2010, *Time* magazine ran a lengthy article about the undisclosed relationship between Avandia, a diabetes drug, and heart attacks. The article used Avandia as a case study of continuing flaws in the drug approval process, and explained how the Avandia issue came to light:

> "Then came a bit of legal serendipity. As part of a settlement with the state of New York over GSK's nondisclosure of possible heightened suicide risk among teenagers taking its antidepressant Paxil, the company agreed to put all its recent clinical studies on a website. Aware of the growing concerns among clinicians about the risks posed by Avandia, in April 2007, Cleveland Clinic cardiologist Dr. Steven Nissen Googled the site and downloaded all of the available Avandia trials. After analyzing the 42 trials, he wrote up his findings and in May submitted them to the *New England Journal of Medicine*. He had found what GSK and the FDA already knew: a 43% higher rate of cardiac events among Avandia patients compared with those taking other drugs or placebos."

But just as with the analyst cases, the question that bothered me was this: Where were the self-regulatory forces that we were supposed to be able to rely upon? Had there been a single murmur from any pharma entity questioning the false claims of any drug marketed by the companies? Had there been standards enunciated designed to prevent the false claims? Had there been a statement requiring that all negative correlations and side effects be revealed? The answer of course, was no.

Once again, self-regulation had been shown to be a complete sham.

What was just as remarkable as Glaxo's behavior with respect to Paxil, perhaps, was the response of those who would always seem to defend corporate impropriety. *The Wall Street Journal*, in an editorial on June 21, 2004, said that our suit was threatening "to damage good science and public health." After maligning the hard facts in our complaint, and accepting the outright misrepresentations of Glaxo, *The Journal* noted that "the process is working exactly as it should." I guess covering up dangerous correlations with adverse side effects is what *The Journal* editorial board considers to be working properly.

Self-regulation, of course, also fails in the public sector. Our experience with governmental watchdogs over ethics abuses has been that they have almost universally failed to ferret out wrongdoing, or act properly when it is apparent. This short tale is demonstrative.

THE ALBANY LOBBYING

COMMISSION

AND PHILIP MORRIS

One small vignette relating to Albany and ethics "self-regulation" makes it clear that the same issue troubling Wall Street and big pharma relate as well to our political world. Albany's ethics laws were porous, to say the least, and the entity that existed to enforce them in 1999 was, quite frankly, weak beyond description. The failure to dig meaningfully into Philip Morris' lobbying misdeeds makes this evident—and once again proves that self-regulation, in any context, is almost surely not going to work.

On July 27, 1999, *The New York Times* published an article summarizing hundreds of internal Philip Morris documents that described Philip Morris' lobbying expenses in Albany from 1993 through 1996. These documents were some of the confidential tobacco company documents made public through the settlement of the multi-state tobacco litigation initiated by the state Attorneys General. They provided a window into the breadth of tobacco lobbying, and made it clear that at least 115 then-current and former members of the New York State Legislature, as well as public officials in the executive branch of the state government, had accepted gifts from Philip Morris, including sporting events, concert tickets, and expensive meals.

Under the state's ethics law in effect at the time, legislators were unable to accept gifts valued at more than $75 on any one occasion if the gifts were intended to influence a decision. The difficulty of proving this "intent," of course, made it difficult to prove the illegality of these gifts. In fact, no legislator had been penalized for receiving illegal gifts since the institution of the ethics laws in 1987. A smarter law would have simply banned the gifts, whether or not there was an intent to affect the outcome of a decision.

In addition to raising issues of the compliance of legislators with the state ethics law, the article also accused Philip Morris of not complying with state lobbying laws in disclosing the amount of money they used to lobby lawmakers—and indeed of falsifying those documents to make it appear that the amount spent fell below the permissible thresholds. It seemed that Philip Morris had used all sorts of clever—and not so clever—means to skirt the disclosures.

On August 16, 1999, Philip Morris announced, "We are in the process of reviewing our previous filings to determine whether any need to be amended in order to bring them into full compliance with the law."

Under the lobbying disclosure guidelines, lobbyists were required to report all gifts as an aggregate sum and itemize any that exceed a value of over $75. In one type of deception, Philip Morris' Albany lobbyist, Sharon Portnoy, had falsely inflated the number of people at a dinner to bring the per person value below the permissible $75 limit. As a result, Portnoy could claim she was not required to report such gifts. It was clear this was a can of worms waiting to be thoroughly investigated.

On November 12, 1999, the Lobbying Commission announced that Philip Morris had agreed to a settlement that included a $75,000 fine and a three-year ban on lobbying imposed on Portnoy. She was also fined an additional $15,000 and Philip Morris agreed to be subject to unannounced audits over the next three years. Philip Morris admitted to violating the state lobbying disclosure laws fifteen times over three years by under-reporting lobbying expenses.

David Nocenti, my extraordinarily wise counsel, and I believed that the Lobbying Commission's settlement with Philip Morris was a mere slap on the wrist—and I said so publicly. We knew from years of experience investigating wrongdoing that a thorough investigation would reveal much more. Leads abounded yet had not been followed. We also believed that the Commission should have referred the matter to our office for prosecution. As a matter of law, without the referral, we had no jurisdiction. On November 15, 1999, I wrote a letter to the Commission formally requesting such a referral, and also identifying why the Commission's action, as structured, was inadequate. Among the failures, the Commission failed to determine if anyone more senior than Portnoy even knew about the falsification of records—or had countenanced it. Shortly thereafter, David and I had a heated conversation with David Grandeau, the executive director of the Lobbying Commission, in which we asked him to refer the matter to us for inquiry. He refused. His refusal made no sense from a prosecutorial perspective.

Yet ten years later it all made sense. Grandeau came to my office seeking to raise money for his newly created charitable entity. I raised the issue of his refusal to make the referral—and he laughed. "Joe wouldn't have wanted the referral," is what he said. Joe, of course, was Joe Bruno, the powerful Albany politician and at that time the president of the state Senate. I asked him why that mattered. Grandeau responded that Bruno had been the one who arranged for him to serve as the executive director of the Commission, and he thought it was his obligation not to make a referral that Joe would not have supported. So there it was: Grandeau—who in my mind had always been viewed improperly as an independent voice—had been willing to refuse to make a referral that would have opened a window into one of many lobbying abuses in Albany, because Joe Bruno didn't want the investigation done. So much for Grandeau's independence from the very people he was supposed to investigate!

Bruno has since been convicted of federal corruption violations. The indictment is worth reading. Even though his conviction was reversed on a technicality, the Second Circuit Court of Appeals is now deciding the merits of his effort to avoid a retrial.

Self-regulation is no more than the fox guarding the hen house. That was the common thread running from Wall Street analysts, to big pharma, to Albany ethics. It is all the same—all hiding behind the pretense of self-regulation, hoping nobody takes a real look at what is going on.

4

FIDUCIARY RULES

Rule Four:

Respecting fiduciary duty is the key

to integrity, and our economy, yet it is

too often observed in the breach.

Our economy was once dominated by small, individually owned companies doing business directly with other companies of similar scale. These entities, owned by neighbors and friends, were all part of closely knit communities of shared values and interests. Now, our economy is dominated by huge multinational corporations and mammoth government agencies—all supposedly acting on behalf of large groups of customers, shareholders or the public. This transformation has forced us into a world where "agency relationships" are the key. That's a pretty dry term. What it means is that people and businesses are often no longer just acting on their own behalf; they are supposed to act in the best interest of others—those whom they represent.

The obligation to act as an agent in the best interest of somebody else is what lawyers generally refer to as a "fiduciary duty." A fiduciary duty is supposed to be sacred—if you violate it, you violate your solemn bond to act on behalf of the other person. Yet succumbing to the temptation to act in one's own self-interest as opposed to the best interest of a client, customer, shareholder, or constituent is what has led to the degradation of fiduciary relationships. And those violations of fiduciary duty are at the core of all the stories we have encountered: in government, the private sector, the not-for-profit world. Virtually every one of the cases we have discussed, and will discuss, comes back to a violation of this central obligation: the stock analyst who lied, the insurance broker who deceived, the politician who undermined democracy.

Fiduciary duties stand at the very vortex of our economy—at the very core of how our financial system is supposed to operate. If fiduciary duties are respected, things work fine. If they are violated, we get crises like the cataclysm of 2008. The problem we have faced—reduced to its greatest simplicity—is that conflicts of interest were baked into so many of the business models at our largest financial entities that respect for fiduciary duties dissipated and the core integrity of our economy caved. The complexity of our financial structures made respect for these fiduciary relationships ever more complicated, making it possible for people to confuse what their true obligations might be—often intentionally of course.

This sad saga is further evidence of Senator Daniel Patrick Moynihan's brilliant theory of "defining deviancy down." We failed to object to corrosive behavior that we should have recognized at every step to be unacceptable. This led ultimately to an overarching failure of our standards of conduct. Values declined bit by bit, like barnacles accumulating on the bottom of a boat. Each step or violation seemed small. Individually they didn't seem to matter all that much; yet in the long run they destroyed the entire structure.

Of course, as many will rightly point out, the respect for fiduciary obligations has slipped everywhere, not just in the financial sector. It is perhaps part of the overarching moral decline some have claimed to see, whether it is accurate or not. In this chapter we will look at fundamental violations of fiduciary duty in multiple sectors: the public, private, and not-for-profit. The problem in each sector is the same. And no, I am not blind to the fair claim that I in a very public way failed to respect a fiduciary obligation that is perhaps even more central. So I make these observations with that reality very much in mind.

A revealing story: Several years back, when my daughters were about 10, 12, and 14, sitting around the dinner table one Sunday night, I made an effort to get a conversation going. I said to them: "So what is your favorite word?" My eldest daughter rolled her eyes, as only a teenager can, looked at me with some despair, and said: "Daddy, that is a pathetic way to get a conversation going. I don't have one, but I do know what yours are." Curiosity sparked, I asked, a bit concerned, "So, what might they be?" And she said: "Fiduciary duty." It was somewhat disheartening, but at the same time it made sense. After all, the girls had heard me talk so much about the violations on Wall Street and elsewhere that they had come to realize that the common thread—the common words that bound it all together—were "fiduciary duty."

The analysts cases I described above were perhaps the first of our "mega cases" where the violations of fiduciary duty emerged: The analysts had a duty of truthfulness to the clients to whom they were recommending stocks, but violated that duty in order to garner the fees, bonuses, and future investment banking business that would result from placing a buy on the stocks—regardless of the underlying merit of the recommendation. But that case was merely the first of many.

One other story before we dive into the sordid tale of mutual fund fees—perhaps the largest middle-class rip-off we tried to remedy in my years as Attorney General. This story relates to a government failure: the selection by the New York State Legislature of a State Comptroller. What does that have to do with fiduciary duties? It demonstrates how the overarching issue of fiduciary duties and the ease with which we now ignore them spans all sectors.

THE LEGISLATURE: KEEPING ALL THE TOYS FOR

ITSELF V. HONORING FIDUCIARY DUTY

S hortly after I was elected Governor, the incumbent New York State Comptroller, Alan Hevesi, resigned. Pursuant to the state Constitution, the Legislature had the responsibility of choosing a replacement. Because Hevesi had resigned almost immediately after he had been elected, the term to be filled was for virtually the entire four years. This is a position of enormous import—not only because the Comptroller has the authority for auditing the entirety of state government and certifying that the budget is in balance, but also because the Comptroller is the sole trustee of state pension funds that exceed $160 billion in value. As a consequence, the Comptroller is one of the most important individual decision-makers with respect to public finance, equities, and debt, and is theoretically among the most important voices on issues ranging from shareholder rights to corporate governance to management of our nation's biggest companies. The state Comptroller is perfectly positioned to lead the much-needed revolution in corporate governance— but more on that later on.

Consequently, I met with the Speaker of the State Assembly, Sheldon Silver, and the Majority Leader of the Senate, the same Joe Bruno—positions that are the equivalent of the Speaker of the House and the Senate Majority Leader in Congress—and suggested that we come up with a way to choose the best possible Comptroller. Historically, the Legislature has chosen one of its own members for elevation in such circumstances—essentially refusing to consider those not in the legislative club. I suggested instead that we let an outside panel of former Comptrollers, all eminently respected and also politically savvy, deliver a list of up to five individuals to the Legislature, and the Legislature would then choose from that list. Both Shelly Silver and Joe Bruno agreed. To some fanfare we issued a public statement announcing the formation of the screening committee. The agreement was viewed as significant evidence of the Legislature's willingness to change the manner in which it conducted business.

The statement said clearly that the committee would send its list of "up to" five members to the Legislature. Here is the critical passage: "The comptroller screening panel, composed of people with longtime experience in government and finance, will review the credentials of those seeking the position and produce a short list of most-qualified candidates for the legislature to consider. ... At the conclusion of the process, up to five comptroller candidates will be selected and these names will be made publicly available."

I and the public were satisfied that the process would create an opportunity for qualified and experienced candidates to be viable contenders. The process would not be limited merely to consideration of members of the State Assembly. As a consequence, I successfully encouraged a number of serious finance pros to throw their hats in the ring.

When the committee of "experts" reported back its list, it had three names on it—and not one of them was from the Legislature. At first blush it seemed that our process had worked: Merit would determine the outcome, not politics. Immediately, however, I got panicked calls. Joe and Shelly had assumed that inevitably the committee would place a member of the Legislature on the list, and that individual, thus blessed, could be voted in and all would be happy. But the committee, demonstrating the independence and judgment we had asked of them, applied its best judgment with respect to the qualities needed for the office—market wisdom, financial savvy, managerial skill—and decided that the members of the Legislature who had applied did not satisfy these parameters.

Hence the crisis. Immediately Shelly and Joe began to seek a way out—first claiming that the failure to name five candidates was a violation of the obligation of the screening committee, though it clearly was not. Then they simply challenged the validity of the committee. The problem became apparent when the time for a vote drew close. Tom DiNapoli—a good friend, a legislator of many years standing, and someone whom I had thought to ask to be Environmental Commissioner, yet someone not deemed by the screening committee to be worthy of the Comptroller position—was the odds-on choice among the Assembly, and Shelly had the capacity to corral enough votes to assure his winning.

In a meeting with Shelly—just the two of us—I asked Shelly if he would want Tom to handle and oversee Shelly's pension. He responded immediately and forthrightly: "Of course not." Why, then, I asked, should Tom oversee the pensions of all the pensioners in the public system in New York State? Tom—a lovely guy—simply didn't have the critical market expertise needed for this job, especially when the possibility or market turmoil was facing us.

This was the conundrum. Legislators faced a choice: Their fiduciary obligation called for them to select the best candidate they could—the candidate with the skills and expertise in the requisite areas. Yet the desire to claim the prize of a powerful statewide office as something that they could dispense to one of their own members was tempting, perhaps irresistible. To pick someone not based on merit, however, would be a breach of their fiduciary duty. This was the classic test of loyalty to fiduciary duty: honor broader obligations to a defined constituency—the public—or cave to one's desire to appease self-interest and give a job to a friend and colleague.

Indeed, on the floor of the state Legislature, when explaining their votes, many members made it very clear that what motivated their decision was the sense that the position was theirs—it belonged as a piece of chattel to the Assembly to dispense to one of its own. There was not an argument that Tom had better financial skills, would manage the pension funds with greater savvy, or would have greater market acuity. No: the argument was simply that the job was theirs to dispense, and one of their own should get it. Moreover, the participation of a Governor or outside experts who had weighed in on the relative abilities of the candidates—even as part of an agreement with the leaders of the Legislature—was seen as an encroachment on their turf.

The vote was not even close: The members of the Legislature placed institutional loyalty above the interests of those to whom they owed the duty—the public.

My commentary after the selection was harsh with respect to the Legislature. I was quoted as saying: "You have just witnessed the insider game of self-dealing that unfortunately confirms every New Yorker's worst fear and image of all that goes on in the legislature of this state." A *New York Times* article read as follows:

> "Mr. Spitzer said that in recent days he had been asking lawmakers this question: 'If Candidate X—take Tom—were approaching you and saying, "You know what? I've never done this before. Never invested a penny. Never made an asset allocation decision. Don't know a swap from a derivative. But I'm setting up a money management firm tomorrow. I want your pension money to be my first investment. Will you give me your pension to start with?"' 'Nobody said they would,' he said. 'Nobody. That, to me, is dispositive. They wouldn't do it with their money. But they'll do it with the public's money.'"

Editorial boards echoed this precise sentiment: *The Times* said: "With yesterday's choice of a new comptroller, the New York State Legislature failed to select the best candidate for the job. Instead, lawmakers—particularly the Assembly Speaker Sheldon Silver, and his Democratic majority—stuck to their conviction that the position belonged to them. ... The choice is a setback for a legislature that is already considered one of the worst in the nation." The *New York Post* echoed, "Silver and Bruno had promised to select a comptroller from a panel's list of recommendations—and the Long Island lawmaker's name was not on that list. What happened was a disgrace—but sadly no surprise. Clearly, Silver and Bruno would keep their word *only* if the panel nominated one or members of the corrupt Albany Legislature. It didn't—so to hell with the deal." And the *Albany Times Union*: "Take that, New Yorkers. It's what the state Legislature—and most insidiously, the dominant bloc known as Assembly Democrats—think is best that matters. It's what they want, mainly political reward and advancement for themselves, that comes before the public interest."

THE MUTUAL FUND RIP-OFF

To demonstrate the central role that fiduciary duties can play, and what happens when they are violated, let's take a look at a group of cases we brought that will save investors—mom and pop investors who have placed their life savings in the stock market—literally hundreds of billions of dollars over time. The abuses we targeted were hidden in mutual fund fees.

One overarching observation about mutual funds: They are the vehicle we use to entice middle-class Americans into the market. And rightly so. Mutual funds, especially low-fee index funds, are the perfect way for most investors to participate in the marketplace. There is virtually no way a small investor can consistently outperform the market by picking individual stocks. If you doubt that, take a look at the writings of Jack Bogle, the founder of the Vanguard funds, a brilliant guy, and one of the "good guys" in the financial world. Or read the brilliant *Random Walk Down Wall Street*, by Burt Malkiel—my freshman year econ professor, and a member of the Council of Economic Advisers under President Ford. The inability to outperform the market is the reason low-fee index funds are such a superb way to invest and "buy the market." Even the supposedly all-knowing hedge funds have failed to beat broad stock market averages over the past four years!

There is also another—perhaps more theoretical—way to think about the mutual fund cases: Mutual funds are Exhibit A in our effort to democratize the market, by inviting the middle class to invest. Yet we didn't democratize the rules to protect our new investors. Let me explain.

It is accepted wisdom that the creation of the middle class was one of the great accomplishments of the first three-quarters of the 20th century. Wealth was created and shared with a greater and broader segment of society than ever before. The creation of the middle class was a result of a confluence of rising wages, increasing home ownership, a broadening industrial sector, and increasing access to education. Perhaps it should not have surprised us that wealth accretion occurred across a broad patch of our nation during this era. For that was the period of U.S. global dominance—we had a near monopoly on the critical inputs that together permitted economic dominion: the rule of law, skilled labor, mass consumption capacity, traditional capital, as in money, and intellectual capital, as in technology creation. No other nation of scale had all of those critical inputs during this era, though increasingly other nations have joined the club.

As we observed and celebrated this rise of the middle class, for whom a home was often the primary initial investment, we took another critical step. We invited the emerging middle class to invest in the capital markets—not only by creating an enormous mutual fund industry, but also by proselytizing in favor of buying individual stocks. We said to the middle class, participate in the capital appreciation that results from ownership of stock in publicly traded companies. And indeed, over time, an increasing percentage of Americans had some ownership stake in the stock market. In 1900 only 1 percent of the population had stock holdings; by 1959 it was 11 percent, by 1989 it was 32 percent, and by 1998 it was 52 percent. This is what I call the democratization of the market.

The stock market, we said to the middle class, should no longer just be the playground of the rich—the F. Scott Fitzgerald crowd of *The Great Gatsby*. Yet the problem was that as the middle class entered, we left in place rules that might have made sense when only large, sophisticated investors were participating, but surely did not when we had invited small investors into the playground. We did not create either a structure of disclosure or education to ensure that that these new investors had the capacity to make wise decisions or to take careful precautionary steps. Our failure to adjust the rules to protect smaller investors explains many of the failures that later occurred.

This tension between the "invitation in" and the rules confronting new investors is what led me to focus on ensuring that we dealt with cases pertaining to less sophisticated investors. They were more likely to be misled by the so-called "wisdom of the street," and were more prone to be easy prey for the guile and self-interest that had come to dominate on Wall Street.

The analyst cases, discussed above, were quintessential examples of the marketplace gone awry. Susceptible to the bait provided by Wall Street analysts, smaller investors who were trying to pick individual stocks were seduced to buy stocks that even the analysts knew were not wise investors. Recall the second defense made by the Wall Street firms: Everybody knows that the analyst recommendations are flawed and are a result of conflicts of interest. Indeed, sophisticated investors might have known this, and discounted the advice of analysts accordingly. But when the major firms ran advertisements touting their analysts and the awards they had garnered, the larger investing public was misled. The "everybody" who knew that the analysts should be ignored were the sophisticated investors of years past, not the general investing public. And Wall Street knew that.

But the largest pool of capital where the middle class was being fundamentally disadvantaged was in the mutual fund industry. Having persuaded most investors not to try to pick individual stocks but to leave that to the professionals, through mutual fund investments, Wall Street was still ripping off small investors. The fees being charged by the companies were huge, usually disproportionate to the performance or services being rendered. These fees were not properly disclosed, and were a result of interlocking boards that did not properly respect their fiduciary duty to the client whose money was being invested. The numbers, especially today, are staggering: $13 trillion in total mutual fund dollars being invested in 2013, with average fees of about 1.4 percent on equity funds and over 1 percent on bond funds, meaning over $100 billion in mutual fund fees being paid; and yet performance of necessity is no more than the market average. Investors are giving away nearly $150 billion just to get the market average—something an index fund could do for a far lower fee.

And, as I explain below, when these cases reached fruition, the SEC refused to recognize the validity of forcing companies to reduce their self-dealing in the way the fees were set. This reflected the blindness, as was so common, of the SEC's understanding of what was actually going on in the marketplace. Even the judge in the case agreed with us that mutual fund fees deserved judicial review—but more on that below.

The relevant point in the discussion about market reform was made (though inadvertently) by a senior lawyer for Fidelity, a member of the panel I was on. She was asked about Fidelity's posture with regard to disclosing how it voted the proxies of shares it controlled. Mind you, Fidelity was, and is, one of the largest shareholders in the market. As of the end of February 2012, granted, several years after the event, Fidelity had over $3 trillion under its control, and $1.6 trillion in managed assets. Of course funds, and the shares they own, are not the managers' per se—they are being held and invested for the millions of investors in their funds. But when asked how they disclosed, or whether they disclosed, the proxies they cast, the general counsel said, "no they did not—it would be too expensive to do so."

I couldn't quite believe what I was hearing. This was a horrendous answer at many levels. First, at a policy level, of course, the proxies cast by a mutual fund on behalf of its investors should be disclosed. So the answer was wrong as a matter of simply transparency. Second, as fibs go, this was an obviously bad one. The cost of posting online how Fidelity cast its proxies was *di minimus*. Even if Fidelity did not want to disclose how it cast its proxies, it needed a better rationale for not doing so. Blaming nondisclosure on cost was simply dumb, and nothing is worse than a bad lie. It exposes both a lack of integrity and a lack of respect for the audience. Had they said there were tactical investment reasons not to disclose, it might have been a bit harder to rebut the argument. But cost was simply an implausible argument.

So the bad fib begged the question: What was the *real* reason they didn't disclose? And the real reason is that mutual fund companies rarely want to vote against management, because management gets to decide whether the mutual fund company will be included on the list of choices for employees to select for their managed retirement accounts. And that flow of investment money is critically important to the mutual fund companies. So who wants to alienate the management? (See "When Your 401(k) Provider Doesn't Vote Your Interests," by Lewis Braham of Bloomberg News.) And of course, this reason for nondisclosure is a violation of the fund's fiduciary duty to cast proxies in the best interest of its investors!

The fundamental point: A mutual fund complex wanted the upside of investing our funds, garnering huge fees, but did not feel an obligation to disclose how it was using our funds to exercise control over the companies it owned—nor was it compelled back then by laws or rules. This is merely one more example of the tension between the invitation to invest that had been extended to the middle class and the rules that have not been crafted to permit middle-class investors to have say or dominion over their own dollars. It is also, of course, one more glaring conflict of interest that remains usually hidden, and also one reason that another vast pool of capital is rarely used to actually affect corporate governance. But more on that in Chapter Five.

The simple point is that there was and still is a chasm between the invitation into the capital markets that we have extended to the middle class, and the rules we have crafted to protect and inform the middle class about the risks they are absorbing. This calls for a fundamental rewrite of the rules, driven by simplicity, clarity, clean language, and a clear obligation of fiduciary duty on the part of those who are supposed to be looking out for the investor. We still have a long way to go in this regard.

But now to the mutual fund cases themselves—which blew the lid of an entire multi-trillion-dollar industry.

Although the case was really in the end about fees, it started with a focus on something arcane called "late trading" and "timing." These improper strategies were designed by hedge funds and mutual funds together—who conspired to siphon off profits that should have gone to mutual fund investors but instead went to hedge funds. There is still no better explanation for the timing and late trading scandal than the first few pages of the complaint we filed against a hedge fund, Canary Capital, on September 3, 2003. The schemes Canary was participating in were emblematic of a vast industry of deceit.

For years before we filed the complaint, Canary engaged in two fraudulent schemes, improperly earning tens of millions of dollars at the expense of mutual fund investors. The schemes involved the complicity of mutual fund management companies that violated their fiduciary duties to their customers in return for substantial fees and other income for themselves and their affiliates.

The first scheme was Canary's "late trading" of mutual fund shares. The daily price of mutual fund shares is generally calculated as of 4 p.m. Eastern, when the market closes. Orders to buy, sell, or exchange mutual fund shares placed at or before 4 p.m. Eastern on a given day receive that day's price. Conversely, orders placed after 4 p.m. Eastern are supposed to be priced using the *following day's* price. This price, known as the Net Asset Value or "NAV," generally reflects the closing prices of the securities that comprise a given fund's portfolio, plus the value of any cash that the fund manager maintains for the fund.

Canary agreed with certain financial institutions (including the Bank of America) that orders Canary placed after 4 p.m. on a given day would illegally receive that day's price (as opposed to the next day's price, which the order would have received had it been processed lawfully). This allowed Canary to capitalize on post-4 p.m. information, while those who bought their mutual fund shares lawfully could not. Late trading is almost like betting today on yesterday's horse races.

The system of 4 p.m. pricing assures a level playing field for investors. Mutual fund investors do not know the exact price at which their mutual fund orders will be executed at the time they place the orders (unlike stock investors), because NAVs are calculated after the market closes. Orders placed on or before 4 p.m. on a given day are filled at the NAV determined that day, while orders placed after 4 p.m. are filled at the NAV calculated the next day. Thus, all investors have the same opportunity to assemble "pre-4 p.m. information" before they buy or sell. And no investor has (or at least is supposed to have) the benefit of "post-4 p.m. information" prior to making an investment decision. The importance of this protection becomes clear when, for example, there is an event after 4 p.m. (like an unexpectedly positive corporate earnings announcement) that makes it highly probable that the market for the stocks in a given fund will open sharply higher the next day.

An investor who has the ability to avoid forward pricing and buy at the *prior* NAV enjoys a significant trading edge. He or she can wait until after the market closes for significant news to come out, such as the above-earnings announcement, and then buy the fund at the old, low NAV that does not reflect the impact of the new information. Taking (legal) advantage of a difference in two prices is called "arbitrage."

Where does the late trader's arbitrage profit come from? Dollar for dollar, it comes out of the mutual fund that the late trader buys. In essence, the late trader is being allowed into the fund after it is closed for the day to participate in a profit that would otherwise have gone completely to the fund's other investors.

The second scheme involved "timing" of mutual funds. "Timing" is an investment technique involving short-term "in and out" trading of mutual fund shares. The technique is designed to exploit inefficiencies in the way mutual fund companies price their shares. Just like late trading, it is widely acknowledged that timing works to the detriment of long-term shareholders and, because of this detrimental effect, mutual fund prospectuses typically state that timing is monitored and that the funds work to prevent it. Nonetheless, in return for investments that will increase fund managers' fees, fund managers often entered into undisclosed agreements to allow timing—for a price.

Because of the adverse effect on investors, mutual funds have employees (generally referred to as the "timing police") who are supposed to ferret out "timers" and put a stop to their short-term trading activity. Many mutual fund prospectuses specifically created the misleading impression that mutual funds were vigilantly protecting investors against the negative effects of timing. In fact, the opposite was true: Managers literally sold the right to time their funds to Canary and other hedge fund investors. The prospectuses, of course, were silent about these arrangements.

As a result of late trading and timing of mutual funds, Canary, the mutual fund companies, and their intermediaries profited handsomely. The losers were unsuspecting long-term mutual fund investors. Canary's excess profits came dollar for dollar out of their pockets.

Canary obtained some of its late trading "capacity" (the opportunity to engage in late trading) directly from one mutual fund manager, the Bank of America. In fact, Bank of America installed special computer equipment in Canary's office that allowed it to buy and sell Bank of America's own mutual funds—the Nations Funds—and hundreds of other mutual funds at the 4 p.m. price until 6:30 p.m. New York time. In return, Canary agreed to leave millions of dollars in Bank of America bond funds on a long-term basis. These parked funds are known in the trade as "sticky assets"—and they generated huge fees for the mutual fund companies.

Mutual fund managers are aware of the damaging effect that timers have on their funds. And while the effects on individual shareholders may be small, their aggregate impact is not: For example, one study estimated that U.S. mutual funds were losing $4 billion each year to timers. (See "Who Cares About Shareholders? Arbitrage-Proofing Mutual Funds" by Eric Zitzewitz.) While it is virtually impossible for fund managers to identify every timing trade, large movements in and out of funds—like those made by Canary—are easy for managers to spot.

Given the harm that timing causes, and the tools available to put a stop to it, why would a mutual fund manager allow a fund to be timed? The answer lies in the way mutual funds are organized. Typically a single management company sets up a number of mutual funds to form a so-called "family of funds." For example, Bank of America Capital Management, LLC, was the manager for the Nations Funds family, including Nations International Equity fund, Nations Small Cap Fund, and so on. While each mutual fund is in fact its own company, as a practical matter the same management company runs it.

The management company makes its profit from fees it charges the funds for financial advice and other services. These fees are typically a percentage of the assets in the fund, so the more assets in the family of funds, the more money the manager makes. The timer understands this perfectly, and frequently offers the manager more assets in exchange for the right to time. Fund managers have succumbed to temptation and allowed investors in the target funds to be hurt in exchange for additional money in their own pockets in the form of higher management fees.

Canary found many mutual fund managers willing to take that deal. Between 2000 and 2003, Canary entered into agreements with dozens of mutual fund families allowing it to time many different mutual funds. Typically, Canary would agree with the fund manager on target funds to be timed and then move the timing money quickly between those funds and a resting place in a money market or similar fund in the same fund family. By keeping the money—often many millions of dollars—in the family, Canary assured the manager that he or she would collect management and other fees on the amount whether it was in the target fund, the resting fund, or moving in between.

These arrangements were never disclosed to mutual fund investors. On the contrary, many of the relevant mutual fund prospectuses contained materially misleading statements assuring investors that the fund managers discouraged and worked to prevent mutual fund timing.

The filing of this complaint, needless to say, was viewed as a major blow to any perceived integrity to Wall Street's appeal to middle-class investors. Analysts could not be trusted, and now even mutual funds were cheating their investors!

The violations of fiduciary duty were at multiple levels. The hedge fund was bribing the mutual fund to violate its fiduciary duty; the mutual fund managers were violating their fiduciary duty by permitting both late trading and timing, thereby diluting returns to ordinary long-term investors; and the management team that oversaw the entire complex of funds was violating its duty to the individual mutual funds by permitting all of this to occur—and also by charging fees that were not negotiated in an arm's length transaction with the fund itself.

Two people were central to cracking these cases. First was Noreen Harrington, a whistleblower whose call to us came out of the blue. A former Goldman banker and thereafter an employee of Canary Capital, she simply could not abide what she had seen in the trenches. Interestingly, she came to us, she said, because she simply didn't think the SEC would do anything with the information she had.

A thin, spritely woman, whose demeanor bespoke a meticulous attention to detail, she was at first met with a degree of skepticism and doubt—almost necessary when anybody brings significant allegations about structural fraud. But I can safely say that not a single claim Noreen ever made was proven to be other than 100 percent accurate. She was a truth teller—to the core. And without her, none of these cases would have been made.

The second person was David Brown, a law school classmate, though not somebody I knew until he joined the AG's office in 2003. He was recommended to me by Carey Dunne, another law school classmate with whom I had worked at the Manhattan DA's office. Carey went on to become one of the managing partners at Davis Polk and the president of the Bar of the City of New York—establishing himself as one of the deans of the legal community in NY.

Carey said to me that David, who was working at Goldman on 9/11, was itching to do something more meaningful, and wanted to "switch sides." I was the lucky one to have snagged someone with the acuity and understanding of the street that David brought with him. Before even joining the AG's office, David had decided to focus on the enormous fiduciary problems posed by management companies in the mutual fund context. He was persuaded that mutual fund managers took huge fees that were not properly negotiated.

The allegations that Noreen provided to us gave us the perfect vehicle to pursue these concerns. The Canary complaint, and the cooperation agreement that I negotiated with Eddie Stern, who ran Canary Capital, broke open an entire cottage industry of hedge funds that were purchasing timing capacity, which had invaded many of the major mutual funds. The losses from the timing were huge, but the much bigger issue, of course, was the lack of real competitive bidding when the fee structures at mutual funds were negotiated. As I testified shortly after we announced the Canary case—95 million Americans from 54 million households paid more than $70 *billion* in advisory and management fees to mutual funds in 2002. If these fees were inflated by at least 10 percent—and we believed it to be much more—then we were talking about a minimum of a $7 billion a year rip-off. The reason for this failure of arm's length negotiation over mutual fund fees was simple and obvious: Interlocking boards were only pretending to negotiate with each other. As I said in my testimony to the Senate: "Our continuing investigations reveal a systematic breakdown in mutual fund governance that allowed directors and managers to ignore the interests of investors. In fund after fund, what we have seen is the wholesale abandonment of fiduciary responsibilities."

David realized that the timing and late trading violations gave us the levers to drive fees down, and to force mutual fund management companies to abide by the fiduciary obligations they had been avoiding.

The industry and the SEC screamed, as they typically did. Giving voice to the status quo, the SEC refused to recognize either that the real issue was the exorbitant fees being charged or that the remedy of addressing the fees was important to ordinary investors and was ripe to be investigated.

The many investigations that the Canary plea and cooperation agreement triggered followed a predictable course: First we established that the fund had been willing, as had been Canary, to let hedge funds use the fund as a vehicle for timing and late trading, contrary to the claims in their prospectus. Then we would negotiate an agreement on restitution to investors and prospective fee reductions. It all became formulaic over time, but much screaming and shouting occurred along the way.

At the end of the day we entered into numerous settlements, about timing and late trading, most also requiring fee reductions and governance changes. Mutual fund investors saved tens of billions of dollars. This was perhaps the largest consumer rip-off I had ever encountered—all because of a breakdown of respect for fiduciary duty.

At a recent political event I ran into Matt Fink, who in 2003 was the president of the Investment Company Institute, the lobbying organization for the mutual fund industry. We laughed over the following small coincidence from a decade earlier: In the middle of August 2003, on the way to a vacation on the outer banks of North Carolina, I and my family had stopped to spend the night at my sister's house in Washington. The next morning, I went out to hit some tennis balls on a public court with a friend. A fellow came over from the adjacent court, and introduced himself as Matt Fink, the chief lobbyist for the mutual fund industry. I innocently asked how his summer had been, and he said "great—you are not investigating us." I said—without any real inflection—"Just wait." We both laughed. I knew he would find out otherwise several weeks later. As it turns out, he heard something in my voice—at least he claims—and was not totally surprised when the Canary complaint was filed.

If the fiduciary relationship was sacrificed by the Legislature in picking a Comptroller, to preserve their own authority, and by the mutual fund companies to pad their own pockets, so too it has been ignored in the not-for-profit world! Herewith the story of the Reader's Digest board.

READER'S DIGEST:

THE POWER OF

MAINTAINING CONTROL

L est you think that violations of fiduciary duty are limited to the private sector, where the craven desire for profit overrides the duty that is required (think of the mutual fund cases or the analysts cases), or the public sector, where the desire to maintain power is the motive (think the selection process for Comptroller or gerrymandering), here is a tale of fiduciary violations in the NOT-for-profit sector. While most not-for-profit organizations serve the interests of the public and of their clients and beneficiaries honorably, our hope that only pure motives reign in that sector is unfortunately not borne out by the record. In telling this tale, I will cut through a slew of complexities to reduce the story to the core essentials.

Reader's Digest (RDA) once was a thriving and powerful publishing empire, among the most influential and august in the nation. It recently went bankrupt for the second time in five years. As with many publishing companies, it faced the treacherous dislocation of new technologies that reduced demand for actual printed content, and RDA also faced the particular problem of an aging consumer base—leaving it with a business model that didn't work. But our issue with RDA was not a story of facing new technology, but how the board of RDA also did harm to the charities to whom they owed a special duty—for what we were convinced were improper and selfish reasons.

RDA was founded by an amazing couple, Lila and DeWitt Wallace. Childless, they left (all) of the stock of RDA to a series of foundations that through several intermediaries contributed the proceeds of this vast bequest to well-known charities, mostly in NYC, from the Metropolitan Museum of Art to Memorial Sloan-Kettering to the Metropolitan Opera.

The problem was that the board of the *for-profit* (RDA) and the *not-for-profits*—what we will call collectively the Foundation—were nearly identical, and inextricably linked. Seven members of the RDA board, including the CEOs of the for-profit and not-for-profit, as well as an attorney and a major banker for the for-profit entity, also served on the eight-member Foundation board.

And this led to a massive confusion on the part of the board members about what their fiduciary duty to the charities required of them.

And here is why: When the for-profit RDA went public, the charities ended up holding in their portfolios almost nothing BUT the shares of RDA. The board of the for-profit RDA kept the stock in the hands of the charities—which they controlled—presumably because this enabled them also to ensure their own continued control of the for-profit: They controlled how the Foundation would vote its shares in all contexts. In order to effectuate this, the board members of the RDA could not permit the charitable entities to sell their RDA stock; if the Foundation sold more than a bit of its stock, then more than 50 percent of the stock of RDA would have been in the hands of public stockholders, whom they did not control, and their total control of the for-profit would have been in jeopardy.

The interlocking boards managed the for-profit and the Foundation neither for the benefit of the charitable beneficiaries, nor the benefit of the RAD investors, but rather for the benefit of the insiders.

This desire to assure themselves continued and absolute control was not injurious to the charities while RDA was thriving, as it did through much of the early 1990s, hitting a valuation of $56 a share in 1992. But as RAD began to fade, the shares tumbled in value, even as the broader market performed brilliantly, and RDA stock fell to $16 by 1998.

The impact on the Foundation and on its designated charities was huge. The fact that they were essentially obligated to merely watch as the stock fell, meant that the Foundation's portfolios and endowments, as well as the dividend revenues that were designated to go to the charitable beneficiaries, also plummeted. Anybody upholding a fiduciary obligation to the charities would have told them to diversify their portfolio—and forced them to so they could limit their exposure to one at risk company and also benefit from broader marker appreciation. But as I said, the RDA board did not do that: They kept their lock on control.

For the charities this meant seriously declining annual support and a bleak future. They were tethered to a sinking ship—with no escape raft being permitted. As a New York Times article in 1997 observed: "To be sure, the Wallaces' beneficiaries would be sitting pretty if the foundations they all depended on had parlayed more of the Reader's Digest stocks into other assets. The stock market has been kind to foundations that were fortunate enough to own a smattering of domestic stocks. For instance, the Ford Foundation's assets rose 8 percent, to $8.1 billion, in 1996, the most recent figures available, while the Rockefeller Foundation's holdings climbed 10.2 percent, to $2.8 billion, in that year." The growth in value for these endowments stood in marked contrast to the multibillion-dollar losses suffered by the beneficiates of the Wallace Foundation funds.

We saw this unfolding, and acted mostly because of the work of an intrepid and special attorney who joined the charities bureau when I came to the office. Marla Simpson, assisted by James Siegel, took on this quagmire. Articulating a theory that the board's act violated their duty to the charitable entities, Marla urged that our office intervene to require a new board, structured to be independent with clear lines of obligation.

A result was a new board, the right to sell the RDA stock, and a massive distribution of wealth to the charities. The May 4, 2001, settlement led to $1.7 billion being distributed to the beneficiaries:

Metropolitan Museum of Art	$424 million
Macalester College	$303 million
The Wildlife Conservation Society	$191 million
The Colonial Williamsburg Foundation	$155 million
Scenic Hudson	$115 million
Open Space Institute	$115 million
Memorial Sloan-Kettering Cancer Center	$100 million
The Metropolitan Opera Association (Lincoln Center)	$92 million
The New York City Ballet (Lincoln Center)	$65 million
Lincoln Center Theater (Lincoln Center)	$59 million
The New York City Opera (Lincoln Center)	$59 million
The Philharmonic Symphony Society of New York (Lincoln Center)	$26 million
The Chamber Music Society of New York (Lincoln Center)	$13 million

The organizations were also now free to sell the RDA stock—and invest wisely. And so they did. I said at the time: "The charitable entities that will receive the money will now be in position to control their own fate and pursue their charitable ends in their own way without being dependent in any way on control by readers digest."

As RDA stock over the years continued its unfortunate decline toward zero, the charities were able to prosper by diversifying away from RDA.

From our perspective, we established that the AG—as the overseer of charitable beneficiaries—could ensure that a board remain loyal to its fiduciary obligation to the charity, and not be subverted by a collateral and improper motive to entrench itself.

I said earlier that in some ways the challenges of not-for-profit governance were more difficult that those facing for-profits. There is a simple reason: As weak as shareholder rights may be, in the not-for-profit world there are *no* shareholders. There is no voice at all pushing back against entrenched management. When we get to a discussion of the Grasso case, recall that the NYSE was a not-for-profit, and there had been no meaningful oversight—until we intervened.

Never forget, violations of fiduciary duty can occur in every sector one can imagine—and will.

5

CORPORATE GOVERNANCE

Rule Five:

Corporate governance

can be worse

than traditional politics.

In previous chapters we looked at ways that violations of fiduciary duty and outright fraud led financial services companies—as well as those in other sectors—to run roughshod over the interests of the clients for whom they were supposedly working: Wall Street analysts lying to their customers or mutual fund companies getting huge and often unjustified fees from their investors.

In this chapter we will look at a subspecies of fiduciary violation where we have seen unique problems explode over the last decade—the arena of corporate governance, where CEOs and other senior executives are getting paid huge sums even when their performance is horrendous. Essentially these CEOs are pilfering money from the shareholders for whom they are supposed to be working. The central aspect of the agency relationship that exists between shareholders and management has been broken; the power dynamic between the two almost the inverse of what it should be.

Before we dive into specific cases and stories, a bit of backdrop and theory. Depending who you ask, corporations from the New York Times to Apple to ExxonMobil, producing everything from the newspaper you read to the iPhone you use to the gas you put in your car, are either among capitalism's greatest inventions, stimulating capital accumulation and fostering innovation and economic growth, or a form of dehumanizing excess that permit the violation of basic human rights and freedoms. The truth is far closer to the former than the latter. But it is the case that some of the greatest abuses of law recently have been at the hands of corporations that seem too often to bring out the worst in those who run them, and then provide those same folks with the greatest opportunity for escaping responsibility. The concept of the corporation is pretty simple: A corporation is a legal form designed to permit somebody running a business to raise capital from a far-reaching and changing group of individuals while bringing structured management to the larger entity. The corporate form recognizes the importance of the separation of capital contribution and management. In a corporation, the thousands of shareholders who have invested have ceded management of the company day to day to a professional cadre who are supposed to act on behalf of the shareholders. Significantly, the corporate form allows those who have invested to have a limit on the liability they face—their risk is no greater than the equity they have invested. While the value of the shares may sink to zero, ordinarily there is no risk that goes beyond that value. These rules have permitted the growth of vast enterprises, as thousands have contributed capital in return for a usually, but not always, proportionate share of ownership, while giving management responsibilities to those who are hired to run the shop on a daily basis.

The theory, when stated like this, seems just fine: increased capital formation, a professional management, and limits on risk that permit growth and risk taking. The problem has been that few structures have been as susceptible to violations of fiduciary duty. And few organizations have been as difficult to sanction and punish when wrongdoing occurs.

Why the risk of fiduciary violation? First we need a primer on how corporations work—in theory. Then we need to take a look at how they *really* work. Once you see the huge gap between theory and reality, you will begin to understand the enormous problem we are facing. And a case study a bit later in the chapter will drive the point home.

The theory: Corporations are owned by the shareholders, who, as a consequence, are empowered to elect a board of directors. The board's primary responsibility is to pick a CEO who runs the corporation day to day. The board will also usually be involved in critical corporate decisions relating to fundamental strategy, mergers, major capital investments, or the performance and hiring of senior members of the management team. In doing all this, the board will rely upon the advice and wisdom of several committees it establishes—most importantly the governance, compensation, and audit committees. In both theory and fact, anybody who has been involved with a board of a public company will tell you that the most important decision the board makes is the selection of the CEO. The CEO of course, relies upon the advice not only of those within management—the general counsel and the senior managers—but also to several critical outside voices who render advice: the outside lawyers, outside auditors, and the investment bankers. In theory, the responsibility of these outside groups—whom I will call the facilitators—is to render impartial advice always directed toward a singular objective: pursuing the best interests of the shareholders. In this structure, we can think of the relationships from the board to the CEO, inside managers and outside advisers and then the shareholders as a chain—a sequence of responsible decision making where it is always the shareholders' interests that are supposed to be protected.

So what is the reality? Over time, we developed what has been called the Imperial CEO. Rather than realizing that they were merely the servants of shareholders, CEOs began to assume the prerogatives of ownership for themselves. How did this confusion occur between agent and principal, or servant and master, or fiduciary and principal? It is very simple: Who actually picks the members of the board? Over time, the CEO does. How? By over time controlling the membership not only of the full board itself but also the membership of the nominating committee. Who picks the members of the audit committee? Over time, the CEO does. Who picks the members of the compensation committee? Over time, the CEO does. And who picks the outside consultants who determine how much the CEO should be paid? The CEO does.

The proof that most boards have lost control over CEOs is that, on most boards, the CEO is also the chair of the board! The board in that context cannot be a meaningful check on the CEO. Look at the debate over whether Jamie Dimon, of JPMorgan Chase, should be both CEO and board chairman. No matter how wise you think a CEO might be, if shareholders have been effectively neutered, and the board is subservient, having the CEO serve as chair of the board as well is a poor idea. The argument against separating the two positions is akin to saying that because we thought George Washington was a great and trustworthy President, we should have gotten rid of the concept of checks and balances in the Constitution. Structure must survive individual leaders. (More on all this below when we discuss the Grasso case.)

If the CEO picks the members of the board and the members of each of the relevant committees, and if, because of the way elections are structured, shareholders really have no choice but to affirm the slate of board members presented to them, is it any surprise that corporate shareholder elections are not in any meaningful way dissimilar from elections in Soviet Russia? Much has been written about quiescent boards, board abdication, and CEO dominion over the very body that is supposed to be the critical check on CEO power. (See *Corporate Governance*, by Robert A.G. Monks and Nell Minow; and "Sarbanes Oxley's Unfinished Business: Abolish the Imperial CEO!" by Jeff Green.) These critiques are apt—and the failure of democracy in the corporate sector has been perhaps more egregious than the failure of process we have seen in the traditional world of politics. At least in the political world we have had two competing parties. In the boardroom, there really has been only one party with a slate of candidates.

The rules of elections for director are so badly rigged that even when a majority of shareholders have voted against the proposed slate of candidates, the directors get to remain! (See "When Shareholder Democracy Is Sham Democracy," by James Stewart.)

The critical point that has aroused the greatest public ire, of course, is CEO compensation. Outrageous CEO pay has become emblematic of all that is wrong with corporate governance. The inflated pay is even more disconcerting in the context of the lack of increase in average wages: Between 1978 and 2011, according to a report in the *Economic Policy Journal*, worker average compensation rose a mere 5.7 percent; CEO compensation rose a shocking 726 percent. This chart shows the shifting average between CEO compensation and average worker compensation:

CEO-to-worker compensation ratio, with options granted and options realized, 1965–2012

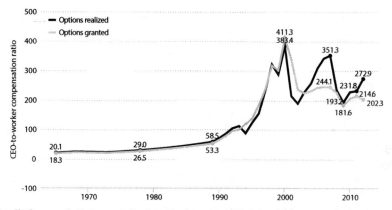

Note: This figure uses the "Options granted" compensation data series which includes salary, bonuses, restricted stock grants, options granted, and long-term incentive payouts for CEOs at the top 350 firms ranked by sales. This figure also uses the "Options realized" compensation data series which includes salary, bonuses, restricted stock grants, options exercised, and long-term incentive payouts for CEOs at the top 350 firms ranked by sales.

Source: Authors' analysis of data from Compustat's ExecuComp database, the Current Employment Statistics program, and the Bureau of Economic Analysis NIPA tables

Although the ratio has fallen since the peak in 2000, does it make sense that CEOs in 2011 were paid 231 times what average workers were, and that this ration has exploded from 20–1 in 1965? Other books have been written just about the failure of the various checks on CEOs—the boards and outside advisers. But my theory is very simple: The CEOs dominate those groups by simply choosing those whom they wanted to serve on the board and hiring those whom they want as advisers.

So I want to ask what I believe is the more fundamental question: What happened to shareholders? They have the final authority, and theoretically they should have been able to escape domination by the CEO.

Just as with our democratic process in the political arena, something must have gone very wrong for the folks who have to get the votes—the CEOs—to suddenly be more powerful than those who in theory control the votes—the shareholders.

Understanding this inversion of power is the real key to understanding the failure of corporate governance: If shareholders were to decide to cast their votes for the people who would truly act on behalf of shareholders, and toss out those who failed to do so, then reform would be possible. The ability of the CEO to choose the members of the board, to dominate the compensation committee, and to pick and choose "facilitators" who will do what they are asked to do, not what they are required to do by their fiduciary duty, would all crumble if shareholders stood up and acted in a way that flexed the muscles they have.

So why don't they? How do we explain the passivity of shareholders? How do we explain the phrase that became ubiquitous in management theory, "passive institutional investors"?

Before we dig deeper to answer this question, we must answer a simple but critical question: Who actually owns the shares of corporate America? It may sound like an obvious question, but the answer is hugely important. The simple answer is "just about everybody." In fact, as discussed in Chapter Four, the percentage of Americans owning stocks peaked at about 65 percent in 2007, before the crash, but has slipped to about 52 percent now. But it is still safe to say that "we own Wall Street"; a big chunk of our nation has some ownership. But the largest pools of these shares are in huge reservoirs controlled by intermediaries: the institutional investors.

We all know that you and I, even though we may own a few hundred shares of stock here and there, really don't have the ability to do anything that will get the attention of a big company. Bear in mind that there are over 8 billion shares outstanding of Microsoft and over 900 million of Apple. So the few shares we own are essentially inconsequential. But there are pools of capital where huge numbers of shares are aggregated and sit in one big reservoir controlled by a few people. So who are these intermediaries who really control the vast pools of shares that could be used to change the direction of corporate management?

For the most part, they are private and public pension funds: U.S. pension funds totaled $16.8 trillion at the end of 2012, with about half of that, close to $8.4 trillion, invested in equities. This is simply a staggering amount of money. About 72 percent of U.S. pension dollars are in private sector pensions—the remaining 28 percent are in public sector pensions.

Pension funds, called ERISA funds for the statute that controls pension investing, are among the most passive shareholders out there. And here is why: Despite the ERISA statute's requirement that the funds be managed for the benefit of the plan beneficiaries, Monks and Minow conclude—rightly—that the funds are ordinarily invested for the benefit of the corporate managers. Not only does the diversity of the holdings of these huge pension funds make any individual case of activism not worth the effort and discomfort, but there is a deeper issue: Since corporate managers often determine how their pension funds vote their proxies, these managers do not want to inspire other companies to vote their holdings adverse to management. All mangers benefit if they are passive. There is almost an unspoken truce among all pension managers: We will not disturb you if you do not disturb us. And indeed that is how it has worked out.

Then there are the folks we were talking about in the last chapter: mutual funds! Of the $13 trillion total they control in 2013, about $4.3 trillion are in equities. Since the total market capitalization of the entire U.S. equity markets is about $17.6 trillion, the mutual fund industry controls about 25 percent of all U.S. equities! That is HUGE. Remember, a lot of this is taken directly from your paychecks and set aside for you to be recovered years from now when you tap into your 401(K). It's held for now in mutual funds—probably ones that you selected—and managed day to day by the mutual funds. Mutual funds traditionally vote with management well over 80 percent of the time on management-sponsored proposals, and rarely if ever support proposals of dissident shareholders. This is hardly a repository of dissident voting!

Endowments, big pools of capital controlled by entities like Harvard, play a big role as well: Harvard's endowment alone was nearly $31 billion at the end of fiscal 2012. These institutions have had major donors over the years and have let those funds grow over time—they are stable, long-term investors whose capital has grown through the miracle of compound interest.

Where, you are wondering, are the avaricious hedge funds we have been hearing so much about in the past few years? They are out there—but they actually control less than the major institutional players. They have averaged about $2 trillion under management over the past few years, and so are not as consequential in terms of sheer size. (They often make up for that by making more noise—just look at the Bill Ackman–Carl Icahn fight over Herbalife!)

Also realize that there is some double-counting here—some pension fund dollars are invested in mutual funds *and* hedge funds!

So that is who has the money. It must strike you that these guys are not the ones who are going to rock the status quo. Other than a couple of the hedge funds, they *are* the status quo. The folks inside corporations who decide how to vote the proxies of the stocks their pension funds own, or the folks who manage mutual funds, are not likely to start throwing out the CEOs of the companies they are in the same country club with—or whose say-so they depend upon to keep control of the 401(k) flow of capital. Remember the story in Chapter Four above, about the answer Fidelity gave about even disclosing how they vote their proxies!

To give you another typical example of interlocking relations that limit independence: The dean of a university with a major endowment also served as the head of the compensation committee of a company whose CEO was the chair of the university's board. The CEO and his company's board were also major contributors to the university. Is there any way in that context that the university is going to vote its endowment shares contrary to the management of the company—or that the CEO isn't going to get a nice boost every year from the compensation committee?

Let's take a short but critical detour into theory. One of the smartest books ever written on management, organizational behavior, and change is Albert Hirschman's *Exit, Voice, and Loyalty*. If anything that follows in the next few paragraphs interests you, read the whole book!

In this short book Hirschman, an economist and a sociologist, explains how people react to any product with which they are dissatisfied. It can be a typical consumer product, a political party, or a company in which they own stock. As disparate as these products may be, the range of possible reactions are really subsumed by the three options named in the title: You exit, leaving for an alternative product provided by a competitor; or you use your voice to persuade the company or supplier of the product to change its offering, trying to get it to pay heed to your complaints; or you remain loyal and usually passive, doing nothing because neither of the other two options appeals to you.

Imagine that you are a customer of a company that makes a classic consumer product—toothpaste. If you decide one day that the product doesn't suit you, it's an easy choice: You pick another product. Have you ever thought seriously about picking up the phone to call Colgate-Palmolive to tell them to change the way they make Colgate? Probably not: The possibility of your having an impact is close to zero; the cost in time and resources too big. It is kind of obvious what the right choice is: Exit. Voice is pointless, and you probably don't have enough Loyalty to remain when the product is unsatisfactory. Good executives, seeing the decline in market share that results from Exit, will try to figure out what is wrong with their products, even if nobody is unilaterally exercising Voice. That is one of the ways markets are supposed to work. Exit produces change over time through market pressure; Voice is likely muted; and Loyalty is a diminished value in something as fungible as a consumer product.

Now, there are times when Exit isn't possible: In a monopoly situation you have nowhere to go. And because companies that have a monopoly usually ignore complaints—precisely because customers have no place to go—the quality of the product will decline over time. A classic case in point is AT&T service before the Bell system was broken up and we deregulated telecom.

Loyalty, of course, is another dynamic altogether, and usually comes into play in determining how people will react to poor performance or a problem of some nature in a family, religious organization, or perhaps a political party. Imagine how tough it is to make the choice to Exit—or even to speak up—in some organizations. The social pressures against vocalizing dissent within a religious organization or a family, or against departing—something we call desertion or even traitorous—can explain why organizations that depend on Loyalty as the glue to bind them together change at such a glacial pace. Pressures to change are tough to find and support.

Hirschman's book plays out the differing reactions and likely responses in the context of the market for different types of goods, as well as political parties. It is worth the time to read the entire volume.

But let's come back to the issue at hand—corporate governance. Imagine you are a typical investor and you own the 100 shares I mentioned above in a company like Apple. Assume you think the company is pursuing policies that are not optimal, or worse. Which of Hirschman's three possible avenues do you pursue, Voice, Exit, or Loyalty?

One of the great positive qualities of our capital markets is what we call liquidity. There are almost always instantaneous ways to sell the shares you own. You can find a buyer by calling a broker—the old-fashioned answer—or by going online to an electronic trading platform. With liquidity almost instantaneous and the transaction costs of trading out of a stock position very low, there is really only one rational option: Exit.

How about using Voice? Can a shareholder with only 100 shares really have any impact? No, of course not. Just as you probably wouldn't call Colgate to complain about the toothpaste, in reality as an owner of 100 shares you probably couldn't get the lowest level lawyer in the counsel's office at a major company to call you back. They would tell you to write a letter and maybe you would get a cursory response from the investor relations department. Is there some other way to exercise Voice? Sure, you can begin to mount a proxy fight. That is one way the rules of shareholder democracy permit owners to begin to apply pressure to corporate leadership. But here is the critical catch: Unless you have a BIG position in the company, the rules of shareholder democracy do not work. It is unbelievably expensive to even begin to launch a proxy effort, and the likelihood of success—even if you had a big position in the company—is close to zero. Why? The rules are stacked against dissident activism. Take a look at the decision by the Court of Appeals for the D.C. Circuit that eliminated a rule that allowed even those who had owned 3 percent of a corporation to nominate an alternative slate of directors! Also see my *Slate* article "The War on Shareholder Activists."

Just look back at the news articles on corporate governance battles. When is the last time a regular, small shareholder was even heard from on any of the issues that are troubling us? I can't recall that it ever happened. So for the small shareholder, Exit is cheap, easy, and puts your capital back in your pocket; Voice is a near impossibility; and Loyalty—just holding your position—of course perpetuates the status quo. So in almost all cases dissenting voices either leave or remain silent.

Let's change the equation just a bit: What if you are Fidelity—or Calpers—or the New York State pension fund; then what do you do if you don't like what a company's leadership is doing? These entities, as the repositories of big stock holdings, have real options open to them: Sure, they *can* Exit. But given their financial depth and their capacity to corral the other major institutions that are the institutional investors—the intermediaries we identified above—they could also use Voice, and lead meaningful efforts to change corporate policy if they chose to do so. But have they? At best, very rarely. Just as small shareholders, they have either Exited or—far more often—remained Loyal. While there have been some exceptions to the rule very recently, my reasonably broad experience suggests that institutional investors are much a part of the problem right now, not the solution. They reinforce the generalized principle of shareholder quiescence, rather than demonstrate a coherent trend line in the other direction. The reasons for this have been studied quite extensively. Take a look at *Are Institutional Investors Part of the Problem or Part of the Solution*, by Ben W. Heineman Jr. and Stephen Davis, for a good overview. Also take a look at "The Giant of Shareholders, Quietly Stirring," by Susanne Craig in *The New York Times*.

My takeaway from actually dealing with many of the leaders of the big institutional investors is that they, like so many others in the corporate world, have simply been socialized into not pushing back. They are comfortable in the social context of dealing with CEOs and do not want to be viewed as being disruptive and trouble makers. The cost—in this context, primarily social—of Voice is still too great. And the financial benefit is too difficult to measure and too diffuse. What I mean by that is that the incremental return to their entire portfolio is so small from waging one proxy fight or disruptive campaign, but the social cost is that their relationship with every company in which they hold stock is harmed. They are viewed as the noisy shareholder, the disruptive Voice, the player who isn't on the team. Since the holdings of these institutional investors are so vast, changing one company's management will have no discernible impact on their portfolio's overall performance.

While the hesitancy of mutual funds to be activist is also driven by the pressure to keep 401(k) funds rolling in, the general passivity of institutional shareholders is more social at root. One can count on the fingers of one hand the number of times that traditional institutional investors have mounted any sort of corporate challenge.

The only possible exceptions to this rule have been a few "renegade" hedge funds, who more often than not cause a momentary change in corporate policy but then are bought out. They have not played any concerted ongoing role in policing corporate governance issues or corralling the role of "Imperial" CEOs.

So Hirschman is correct. Exit, Voice, and Loyalty define the universe of options generally available to a dissatisfied consumer—in this case a shareholder. The easiest options—Exit and Loyalty—have won. And Voice, which has enormous social as well as economic costs, has been largely ignored. The status quo has largely remained intact in this model.

So now let's go way back to the problems of corporate governance: With a CEO who over time begins to dominate every aspect of the chain of corporate decision making, the role of the real folks to whom a duty is owed—the shareholders—has quickly been forgotten, ignored, or minimized.

The lesson is the same as it has been in what we refer to as "traditional" politics: We will get genuine reform only if we return decision-making authority to those who should have the power but whose rights and interests are being forgotten—voters, or in the corporate context, shareholders. The record of the SEC's failures in this regard over many years—beating back efforts to return power to shareholders, while instead listening to the self-interested arguments of CEOs who use the old refrain of "trust us, we know what is in their interest"—is quite appalling.

Let's examine a case that is the paradigm of what happens when a CEO so thoroughly dominates a board and an organization that the decision making takes an unfortunate turn.

THE GRASSO CASE

INTRODUCTION

In the summer of 2003, Richard Grasso had been the chairman and CEO of the New York Stock Exchange for eight years. For that time, Grasso received $210 million in total compensation. From 1999 to 2002 alone, Grasso was awarded more than $80 million in annual compensation, and the value of his retirement benefits increased by more than $80 million. Now, with two years remaining on his contract, he was asking the board to approve a new contract, one that would allow him to take an immediate payout of nearly $140 million in deferred compensation and retirement benefits. As he confided to several directors, he wanted the money now because he was worried that a future board might try to reduce his award.

Grasso had good reason to be concerned. While his retirement benefit, known as the Supplemental Executive Retirement Plan (SERP), had exploded from $36 million in 1999 to $120 million in 2002, the directors of the NYSE had never been told of the increases. Ken Langone, who was the chair of the compensation committee during that time, admitted that he did not know the value of Grasso's SERP until negotiations over the payout began, and the NYSE's board of directors "basically did not monitor or assess the reasonableness of SERP benefits in any way."

As a former vice chairman of the NYSE put it, if Grasso's annual compensation had been disclosed to the members, "they would have hung him," because it was "much too much money."

Indeed, when the compensation committee first learned about the contract negotiations, several members expressed concerns about the size of the proposed payout and requested that an independent consultant be hired to review the proposal. The consultants told the committee that Grasso's compensation and retirement benefits were far above even the most generous comparator and that the early payouts of deferred compensation and retirement benefits that he was seeking were extremely rare and "unusually executive friendly." As more directors learned about Grasso's proposed payout, many expressed shock at the amount Grasso was seeking and urged him to withdraw his request. Grasso responded to these concerns by informing several directors in late July that he would table the proposal.

However, when the board of directors met on August 7, 2003, Grasso's new contract, with its $140 million payout, was still on the agenda. Carl McCall, who had taken over as head of the compensation committee only a few weeks earlier and had not been involved in the contract negotiations, attempted explain to the proposal to the surprised directors. In a chaotic and confused meeting, the board voted to approve the contract, having been wrongly assured that Grasso was entitled to the full payout even if he quit the NYSE that day.

In the days following the August 7 meeting, several directors, including Madeleine Albright, Philip Purcell, and Hank Paulson, tried again to convince Grasso not to take the money, correctly predicting a public relations disaster for the NYSE. Immediately after Grasso's new contract was made public, the NYSE faced a firestorm of questions and criticism that culminated in Grasso's resignation on September 17, 2003, just one month after he had signed the new contract.

BACKGROUND

Dick Grasso's career began and ended at the NYSE. He was first hired in 1968 as a clerk and worked his way up through the ranks to become president and chief operating officer by 1988. He became chairman and chief executive officer in 1995, after being selected by the board of directors to succeed William H. Donaldson, the outgoing CEO and future head of the Securities and Exchange Commission.

Despite its prominence as a symbol of Wall Street, the NYSE during Grasso's tenure was in fact a relatively small not-for-profit corporation. With approximately 1,500 employees and annual revenues of $1 billion, the NYSE was dwarfed by financial institutions like JPMorgan or Goldman Sachs, which had annual revenues of closer to $30 billion and more than 50,000 employees. Moreover, as a New York not-for-profit corporation, the NYSE was subject to state laws that limited the compensation that could be awarded to what was "reasonable" and "commensurate with services performed."

The NYSE during Grasso's tenure served two important functions. Its first was providing a venue for the purchase and sale of stocks. Second, the NYSE was a self-regulatory organization, which meant that it was responsible for enforcing a series of rules designed to maintain a fair and open marketplace. As chairman and CEO of the Exchange, Grasso was responsible for both of these functions.

The Exchange was owned by its 1,366 members, or "seat holders" who could buy and sell shares on the floor of the Exchange. "Specialist" members made markets in particular stocks, matching buyers with sellers and sometimes committing their own capital to ensure that stock prices did not fluctuate too wildly. The NYSE's board of directors comprised 24 directors, the chairman of the board, the executive vice chairman, and the NYSE's president. Directors were nominated by a nominating committee and elected by the members of the Exchange and the NYSE's constitution required that each class of directors consist of six "public" directors and six "industry" directors. Once elected to the board, directors were appointed by Grasso to serve on various committees, subject to approval by the board.

GRASSO'S COMPENSATION

When Grasso became chairman and CEO of the NYSE in 1995, his contract stated that he would receive a base salary of $1.4 million per year, with a target bonus of $700,000. This was in line with the compensation of his predecessor, William H. Donaldson, who was paid $1.7 million in 1994.

From 1995 through 2002, Grasso's annual compensation rose exponentially to a high of $30,600,000 in 2001:

YEAR	SALARY	BONUS AWARDS	TOTAL
1995	$1,260,000	$900,000	$2,160,000
1996	$1,400,000	$1,600,000	$3,000,000
1997	$1,400,000	$3,800,000	$5,200,000
1998	$1,400,000	$4,600,000	$6,000,000
1999	$1,400,000	$9,900,000	$11,300,000
2000	$1,400,000	$25,400,000	$26,800,000
2001	$1,400,000	$29,150,000	$30,600,000
2002	$1,400,000	$10,600,000	$12,000,000
Total	**$11,060,000**	**$85,950,000**	**$97,060,000**

In addition, increases in Grasso's annual compensation had a multiplier effect on his SERP, which was calculated based on years of service and final average pay. From 1995 through 2002, the lump sum value of Grasso's SERP rose from $6.6 million to $120 million. Thus, for the eight years that Grasso was CEO of the NYSE, he received more than $210 million in total compensation; more than $26 million per year. Three different sets of experts concluded that between 70 percent and 80 percent of Grasso's compensation was excessive and objectively unreasonable in light of his responsibilities as chairman and CEO of the NYSE.

GRASSO AND THE NYSE'S FAILURES

Several factors contributed to Grasso's being awarded such excessive compensation, including failures of corporate governance, failures to disclose material information, and fundamental errors in the benchmarks and formulas used to set Grasso's compensation and benefits.

Failures of corporate governance

The first failure that contributed to Grasso's overcompensation was the selection and composition of the NYSE's board of directors and compensation committee. The majority of directors and almost all members of the compensation committee during Grasso's tenure as CEO were subject to regulation and oversight by the NYSE and either they or their firms could be rewarded or punished by Grasso.[4]

Indeed, during Grasso's tenure as chairman and CEO of the NYSE, only a small minority of directors was independent of Grasso, and an even smaller fraction of the compensation committee was independent. From 1999 to 2003, years in which Grasso's compensation more than quadrupled, only one out of six directors and only one out of fourteen compensation committee members was independent of Grasso. Put another way, almost all of the members of the committee responsible for Grasso's compensation had a personal stake in remaining in the good graces of the NYSE's chairman and CEO. In 2001, the year Grasso was awarded more than $30 million, there were exactly zero independent directors on the compensation committee:

2001 NYSE COMPENSATION COMMITTEE	INTEREST
Kenneth Langone—Chair	Securities Firm (Invemed)
Richard S. Fuld	Securities Firm (Lehman Brothers)
Maurice Greenberg	Listed Company (AIG)
Mel Karmazin	Listed Company (Viacom)
David Komansky	Securities Firm (Merrill Lynch)
Gerald Levin	Listed Company (Time Warner)
Robert M. Murphy	Specialist Firm (LaBranche & Co.)
Alex Trotman	Listed Company (Ford)

This composition of the board and the compensation committee did not occur by chance. In another failure of corporate governance, Grasso exerted significant influence over who was elected to the NYSE's board of directors and hand-picked the committees on which directors served. This allowed Grasso to stack the compensation committee with directors who were more likely to approve excessive pay packages, either because of his influence over them or because of a shared interest in ever-rising CEO compensation.

Failures to disclose

A second factor that contributed to Grasso's excessive compensation was a lack of transparency. Every element of information about Grasso's compensation, including his salary, bonuses, Capital Accumulation Plan, and SERP, was withheld from the members of the Exchange who elected the board of directors. Without knowing what Grasso was being paid, members had no means of holding directors accountable for approving Grasso's outrageous pay packages. Moreover, the members of the NYSE were responsible not only for electing directors, but also for paying through membership fees a major portion of the NYSE's expenses. From 2000 through 2002, the amount the NYSE expensed in connection with Grasso's compensation and benefits was equal to 99 percent of the NYSE's net income and comprised over 50 percent of the increases in fees charged to the NYSE's members during those years. Yet the members who nominally owned the exchange and paid membership fees had no way of knowing how well the directors were representing their interests and how much of their increasingly high fees were being redirected into Dick Grasso's pockets.

Additionally, significant portions of Grasso's compensation were not even disclosed to directors. Despite the fact that Grasso's SERP was the most significant single element of his compensation, growing in value by more than $80 million from 1999 to 2002, the board was never told what Grasso's SERP was worth or how much it grew each year. As Ken Langone admitted, the committee "basically did not monitor or assess the reasonableness of SERP benefits in any way." There can be no excuse for Grasso's failure to disclose such material information to the committee and the board.

Each year, the NYSE's compensation consultants prepared estimates of the value of Grasso's SERP, and Langone's predecessor as chair of the compensation committee specifically noted that Grasso's SERP should be disclosed to the full committee. However, neither Grasso nor Langone took any steps to do so. In addition, when the board was asked to approve changes in the compensation structure for the NYSE's nineteen most senior executives in 2001, the value of every executive's SERP, except Grasso's, was disclosed to the board. At that time, Grasso's SERP was valued at $96 million, more than the value of all the other executives' SERPs combined.[5]

Grasso's SERP was not the only element of his compensation that was withheld from the board. When Langone was chair of the compensation committee, the amount of money Grasso received in another form of compensation, called the "Capital Accumulation Plan" or CAP, was literally hidden from the rest of the committee and the full board. The CAP was essentially a second bonus, added on top of an executive's annual incentive compensation award. When CAP was first introduced at the Exchange, Grasso was not eligible for the plan and the CAP awards of his subordinates were displayed clearly on worksheets provided to the compensation committee. In 2000, however, three things happened: Langone took over as head of the compensation committee, Grasso became eligible for CAP, and the worksheets provided to the committee inexplicably stopped displaying the CAP awards.

In fact, the NYSE's human resources department, which prepared the executive compensation worksheets, continued to include a column for the CAP awards, but was directed to hide that column when printing materials for the committee. After Langone presented the altered worksheet and it was approved by the committee, the HR department would "unhide" the column before sending the document to the NYSE's finance department to ensure that Grasso would be paid the proper amount.

Finally, as late as August 2003, when the directors were asked to vote on Grasso's $140 million payout, they were never told that the new contract also provided for an additional $48 million in future guaranteed payments. When the NYSE was forced to disclose these payments a few weeks later, in response to an inquiry by the SEC, many directors were so outraged to learn of the additional payments that even Grasso's agreement to forgo the future payments was not enough to quell the storm. He had lost the confidence of the board and the members of the Exchange and soon resigned.

Errors in benchmarks and formulas used to set Grasso's compensation

The third major factor that contributed to Grasso's excessive compensation was the flawed processes used to benchmark his annual bonuses and to calculate his retirement benefits.

During Grasso's tenure, the NYSE followed a fairly standard practice of using a comparator group to determine establish benchmarks for Grasso's compensation. The purpose of a comparator group is to provide the board with an understanding of the relevant labor market with the goal of avoiding either underpaying employees, which could hurt the organization's ability to retain and attract talent, or overpaying, which would be a waste of the company's assets.

To develop an appropriate comparator group, a company selects a group of other companies that are comparable in relevant ways, such as industry and size. Compensation data is then collected from the comparator group and presented to the compensation committee, typically by reporting the compensation of the median executive within the comparator group and some range by percentile.

The basic flaw in the NYSE's use of a comparator group to set Grasso's compensation was that organizations included in the comparator group were not, in fact, comparable to the NYSE by any relevant measure. The companies used to benchmark Grasso's compensation were on average dramatically larger and more complex than the NYSE. For example, the median annual revenue of firms in the NYSE comparator group was more than 25 times that of the NYSE, the median number of employees was more than 30 times that of the NYSE, and the median assets of firms in the comparator group were more than 125 times the NYSE's assets. As a result, Grasso's compensation was benchmarked not against CEOs of similarly sized not-for-profits performing similar functions to the NYSE, but against CEOs of some of the largest, most profitable companies in the world.[6]

Finally, Grasso was significantly overcompensated even compared to the flawed NYSE comparator group. Not only were his annual bonus awards 25 percent higher than the median of the NYSE's comparator group, but the value of his accumulated SERP in 2002, at $120 million, was larger than that of any other executive in the NYSE's comparator group, or indeed the entire S&P 500 (a group of companies which is, on average, 50 times larger than the NYSE). Compared with CEOs of organizations similar to the NYSE, Grasso's SERP was roughly five times the median.

PEOPLE V. GRASSO

Webb report

Days after Grasso's resignation, the NYSE commissioned an independent investigation to determine how Grasso had amassed such excessive compensation in such a short tenure as chairman and CEO. The investigation was led by former United States Attorney Dan K. Webb and a team of attorneys from Winston & Strawn. After conducting more than sixty interviews, reviewing thousands of pages of documents, and consulting with experts in executive compensation, the team issued what became known as the "Webb report." The report concluded that "Grasso received approximately $144.5 million to $156.7 million in excessive compensation and benefits."[7]

The NYSE's board of directors referred the Webb report to both the Securities and Exchange Commission and to the New York State Attorney General to determine whether further legal action was warranted.

NYAG investigation and complaint

B ecause the NYSE was a New York not-for-profit corporation, the NY Attorney General led the investigation and concluded that the NYSE had violated the New York Not-for-Profit Corporation Law's requirement that compensation be "reasonable" and "commensurate with the services provided." The investigation also concluded that Grasso and Ken Langone had breached their fiduciary duties to the Exchange. The NYAG, on behalf of the People of the State of New York, filed a civil complaint against Richard A. Grasso, Kenneth G. Langone, and the NYSE on May 24, 2004.

The complaint included two independent legal bases for compelling Grasso to forfeit the portion of his compensation and benefits that was excessive. First, under New York law, not-for-profit corporations may pay only compensation that is "reasonable" and "commensurate with services performed." The purpose of the law is to prevent the assets of a not-for-profit corporations being disbursed to the directors and officers, rather than being used to further the stated goals of the not-for-profit. Under this provision of the law, Grasso's compensation and benefits—which from 2000 through 2002 cost the Exchange more than $130 million, or 98 percent of the NYSE's net income over that period—was simply not "reasonable" under New York law.

The second reason to compel the disgorgement of Grasso's excessive compensation was that as chairman and CEO of the Exchange, Grasso owed a fiduciary duty to the Exchange. By implementing and presiding over a compensation process that did not disclose CAP bonuses or SERP awards (including his own), Grasso breached his duty of loyalty and care.

The complaint also charged Ken Langone with breaching his fiduciary duty as chair of the NYSE's compensation committee.

Discovery lasted more than two years, with defendants noticing over sixty depositions and producing over one million pages of documents. With minor exceptions, discovery confirmed the conclusions of the Webb report and the facts alleged in the civil complaint: Grasso's annual compensation had increased exponentially from $2.16 million in 1995 to $30.6 million in 2001; the value of Grasso's SERP had risen from $6.6 million to $120 million; the magnitude and increases in Grasso's SERP had not been disclosed to the board; the information given to the board with respect to Grasso's CAP awards was inaccurate and misleading; and the information given to the board in 2003 with respect to the payout of Grasso's deferred compensation and benefits was also inaccurate and misleading.

Motions

The failure of Grasso and Langone to make their case on the facts was demonstrated when Langone moved for summary judgment, arguing that there was no evidence to support the claim that he had breached his duty to the NYSE. Both the trial court and the Appellate Division denied Langone's motion.

In a subsequent motion by the NYAG, the trial court went even further, holding that Grasso breached his duty to the NYSE by failing to alert the board to his SERP balances. The court stated that as chairman and CEO, "Mr. Grasso's duty is to be fully informed and to see to it that the board was fully informed. He failed in this duty." The court found "shocking" Grasso's argument that he himself did not know the value of his SERP and therefore could not have informed the board. "That a fiduciary of any institution, profit or not-for-profit, could honestly admit that he was unaware of a liability of over $100 million, or even over $36 million, is a clear violation of the duty of care. The fact that it was a liability to an insider (chairman and CEO) is even more shocking and a clear violation of the duty of loyalty."

Despite the clear evidence that both Langone and Grasso violated their duties to the Exchange, neither was ever held to account for their failings, or even to answer to a jury, thanks to a bizarre ruling from an appellate court that had apparently tired of the Grasso case. In September 2008, a divided intermediate appellate court held that the Attorney General no longer had authority to pursue the claims against Grasso because in 2005—two years after Grasso had resigned—the NYSE reorganized into two entities: a for-profit entity that would carry on the NYSE's trading operations, and a not-for-profit that would fulfill the NYSE's regulatory responsibilities. The court found that because part of the NYSE was now a for-profit company, there was no longer a public interest in the NYAG's lawsuit. As the dissent pointed out, the reasoning adopted by the court "would mean that the Attorney General always loses the claim he is expressly authorized to bring…. It would open the door to a feeding frenzy for con men and swindlers to raid assets of not-for-profit corporations they control and then evade prosecution and responsibility by merging with a for-profit corporation."[8] The decision was, as the dissent said, "meritless."

EPILOGUE

Although it is impossible to predict what would have occurred on appeal, given the strong dissenting opinion and the law and facts at issue, there is, at minimum, a good chance that the majority opinion would have been reversed by New York's Court of Appeals. But by 2008, the Attorney General was Andrew Cuomo, who had little interest in pursuing the case. This was made evident in an article Langone wrote for

Bloomberg BusinessWeek, in which he quoted Cuomo as saying to him "we've got to settle this" and then agreeing that the court did the right thing dismissing the case. Horrendous position for an Attorney General to take.

And so Cuomo quietly acquiesced without appeal from an intermediate appellate decision that stripped the NYAG—his own office—of its authority to bring claims against directors of a former not-for-profit. Ken Langone never had to answer for his failure to disclose the full amount of Grasso's compensation to the board or justify the $160 million in total compensation that Grasso was awarded during the four years that Langone chaired the compensation committee. And Grasso was allowed to keep the hundreds of millions of dollars in excessive compensation that he had received without ever answering why, if his compensation was so reasonable and he had not breached his fiduciary duties, the members and directors of the NYSE were so shocked to learn of his pay, that he was forced to resign.

One more story about the NYSE board will drive home how twisted the definition of "public purpose" was during Dick Grasso's reign. The NYSE, by statute, was required to have board members who were to fill different slots: Included among these positions were so-called "public" representatives. These board members were supposed to serve as the voice of "real" people—those who invested and participated in the capital markets as small or more typical investors—not the behemoths of Wall Street. Although the board was dominated by the CEOs of the major Wall Street banks as you have seen, the statutes creating the NYSE required that several board positions be reserved for those who would bring a different and more public-oriented perspective to the board.

So imagine my surprise—and more—one Saturday morning when I picked up The New York Times and read an article that said Dick Grasso was nominating Sandy Weill to be a member of the NYSE board—and that the seat he would fill would be one of those reserved for a public representative! Sandy was the chairman of Citibank—the largest financial entity in the nation at the time, the very bank whose merger had required the repeal of the last vestiges of Glass-Steagall, which had limited the relationships between securities firms and banks. Sandy was also at the time still the subject of our ongoing investigation about the propriety of his and analysts' behavior at Citibank. Plus, his bank had just agreed to pay a $400 million fine for participating in the analyst frauds!

When I read the story, I called the NYSE, and got the 24-hour guard, and asked him to track down Dick Grasso for me. When we talked a few moments later, I was pretty direct. I suggested to him that the appointment was contrary to every bit of common sense, and that making this appointment at this moment would be an act of defiance by the NYSE.

He said he would think about the matter and get back to me. I told Dick I would refrain from saying anything publicly until he had a chance to reconsider.

As it turned out, I was about to get on a plane, so it would be several hours until we could speak again. When I landed, I called Dick, and he said he would not withdraw the nomination. Moreover, he pushed the responsibility for the decision to nominate Sandy to the nominating committee, pretending he had no role whatsoever. Knowing what I did about the way the NYSE operated, and Dick's iron grip on every decision, I viewed this as total nonsense.

I said that was his prerogative, but I felt compelled to make a public statement. And so I did—blasting the horrendous judgment of the NYSE. I called the *Times* reporter who had covered the nominations and was quoted as saying that "To put Sandy Weill on the board of the exchange as the public's representative is a gross misjudgment and a violation of trust. He is the chairman of the company that is paying perhaps the largest fine in history for perpetrating one of the biggest frauds on the investing public. For him to be proposed as the voice for the public interest is an outrage."

Several hours later, Sandy Weill announced that he was withdrawing his name from nomination. The board, led by Grasso, had refused to act; Weill had the good sense to recognize the idiocy of the nomination. This was true to both their characters: Sandy was the consummate deal maker and charming wheeler-dealer; Grasso was stubborn, and simply refused to recognize either the substantive or visual foolishness of the nomination.

***

This interplay in a way summed up all that was ingrown and wrong about the leadership and judgment of the NYSE. And this was the organization that controlled the integrity and central nervous system of our entire market structure. Is it any wonder we have had serious problems with corporate governance?

But is there an answer? I actually think there might be, and it follows from much of what we have discussed in this chapter: Ownership trumps regulation. Even as everything that we have just read proves, ownership doesn't always exercise its rights: The failure of corporate democracy and the failure of institutional investors to use their capacity to impose reform on broken corporations is quite real and one of the tragedies of our corporate world over the past 20 years. Yet there might be a chance to change all that. Because even as there are structural reasons that ownership—the passive institutional investors we discussed above—have failed to fulfill their mandate to oversee corporate governance, it might still be possible to make a vision of genuine corporate democracy a reality.

Clearly, prosecution and regulation have been our first reflexive responses to wrongdoing in the corporate arena. And we have been rightly
frustrated by the near total absence of the former and the failure of the
latter. Perhaps it is time to recognize that reliance upon these two has
become in some ways an intellectual crutch, permitting us to abdicate
the more potent and powerful prerogatives of ownership. At the end of
the day, if used properly, ownership trumps either prosecution or regulation as a mechanism to change behavior; as shareholders, we—the
public—do in fact own the companies and other entities whose behavior we so often deride. Yet we have failed to use the capacity we have as
owners in our society to have an impact on the behavior of those organizations that are most at fault for the debacles of the past decade.

This is not an effort to infuse politics into corporate governance—just
the opposite. It is an effort to ensure that the gross excesses in salaries
and leverage that led to the massive destruction of middle-class wealth
is not repeated. These crises occurred because we—as shareholders—
have failed to place checks on the imperial CEOs who took excess risk
with our funds, pocketing much of the upside but leaving all of us, both
as shareholders and taxpayers, with the downside risk.

Even reasonably good laws—like Sarbanes-Oxley and Dodd-Frank—
and more prosecutions would at best set only broad parameters for behavior, leaving room for the "legal but horrendous" decision making
that can create great harm. Regulation and prosecution cannot ensure
the exercise of good judgment. The wise use of ownership can.

Are there examples of wise owners whom we should emulate? Yes:
Take Warren Buffet. We as shareholders should exercise the same degree of control and oversight that he does with the major companies in
which he is the controlling shareholder. He uses his ownership power to
ensure the exercise of good judgment and sound business practices and
is neither passive nor quiescent. He does this by ensuring that the CEOs
are individuals in whom he has absolute confidence.

Earlier in this chapter we went through who the "we" is that owns these
entities. The vast pools of capital that own the majority of the shares in
our major companies are the mutual funds that are the funds deposited
and owned by tens of millions of middle-class workers and investors,
and the pension funds—public and private—that are the repository of
the retirement accounts of the tens of millions of workers who set aside
the funds for their later years. These pools of capital can and should be
harnessed and used—by those whose money is being invested—to control the companies in which they have invested.

Because we have ceded the prerogatives of ownership to those who
claim to be acting on our behalf—and have too often failed us—we have
failed to live up to our own obligations as owners in society. Those to
whom we ceded this power too often took advantage of our passivity to

pursue unduly risky, self-interested, and sometimes corrupt practices that sowed the seeds of cataclysm and violated the foundations of our market economy.

There is historical precedent for organizing and using the prerogatives of ownership of capital to alter corporate behavior in a fundamental way: in the '70s and '80s shareholder pressure brought to bear on companies investing in apartheid South Africa led to withdrawal of much capital from that regime, and contributed significantly to the end of apartheid. More recently, the pressure on Cerberus by public pension fund investors in that private equity fund led to its quick decision to sell Bushmaster, which produced the semi-automatic gun used in the Newtown massacre.

What is needed is leadership by those who control the pension funds and mutual funds to use their shares in furtherance of good corporate decision making. State and city comptrollers and treasurers have an enormous opportunity to determine how the shares we own through the pension funds they control are used to control the companies we invest in. It is about time that we—as shareholders—got more actively involved, through these representatives, in everything from compensation, to board membership, leverage ratios, and lending practices. There is no reason at all that the only activist shareholders should be a few titans in the hedge fund world.

Another step organized shareholder voices could take would be to overturn the consequences of the Supreme Court decision in the Citizens United case, that the government cannot limit corporations' political expenditures, equating corporations to people. Companies could be required by shareholders to cease political giving and advocacy— to stick to their knitting as it were. Shareholders will reverse Citizens United long before either the Supreme Court or a constitutional amendment will. Shareholder resolutions could be passed saying to management, leave politics to the political arena. Or every proposed political contribution could be disclosed and then put to a shareholder vote. Even if the Supreme Court has said corporations have a right to participate, we as shareholders could tell CEOs that we don't want them to use shareholder assets that way. Focus on building a better car or a more efficient air conditioner. Let those in the political arena be responsive to individual voters. No funneling money into the political world through pseudo-not-for profits or lobbying through the Chamber of Commerce, or the Sierra Club for that matter, without an explicit shareholder vote of approval. Stay out of that game altogether.

And to those who immediately cry, but what about the fiduciary duty of the pension managers to focus exclusively on maximizing return? There is a simple, and correct, answer: This is the best, and indeed, only way to do it in the long run. Ceding power without limits to those who wish to take advantage of shareholder passivity led to cataclysm, not wealth creation.

To the extent the rules of shareholder democracy have been mangled—just as have been the rules of voting in our traditional political arena—we need those rules to be rationalized and brought into balance. And this is a job for Mary Jo White, the new SEC chair: The rules permitting shareholder voice and say must be expanded and guaranteed—not squelched, as the leaders of the Chamber of Commerce have sought to do. Advocacy for this can be led by the major institutional shareholders. Shareholders hold the keys to reformed governance—they must use them and stop blaming the lack of prosecution and regulation for all the ills in our private sector.

6

UNDERSTANDING
WALL STREET

Rule Six:
The Masters of the Universe
win while you lose.

Some of what goes on in the murky world of Wall Street is terribly complex and requires significant mathematical, legal, or accounting skills to understand. But more of what goes on is simple, straightforward, and not terribly pretty. In this chapter we are not going to dive into the complexities of structured investment vehicles—but what I will try to do is give you a better understanding of the psyche and basic motivating forces behind the bubbles that emerge with regularity. And that is much more important. Because beyond the stories from prior chapters, and some of the theory we have already covered, we still need to try to figure out why bubbles seem to inflate with such frequency, and why the small investor is so often on the wrong side of so many transactions. I will not pretend to be original in this critique or diagnosis. There are some stupendous books to draw upon that reveal the way Wall Street has generated its own mythology, avoided true revelation, and yet with great frequency also done things that are neither terribly useful nor honorable. In particular, you should read Simon Johnson and James Kwak's *13 Bankers: The Wall Street Takeover*, and Joe Nocera and Bethany McLean's *All the Devils Are Here*. The problem is not that the critique is not there—it is that we either forget it or intentionally ignore it when the markets are heading up, as they are right now.

Let's start with first principles: Banking, financial services, and the capital markets are all about intermediation—which is nothing more than a fancy word for moving capital (a fancy word for money) from those who have it to those who need it. It sounds quite simple—and it is. The most basic set of banking transactions might look like this: I put money in a savings account; the bank then puts that money together with money other people have deposited into their savings accounts, and lends that money to folks to buy a house. The bank charges the homeowners interest (maybe 5 percent these days) on that loan—which we call a mortgage—and pays the savers (depositors) a part of the interest (let's say 1 percent), keeping the rest for itself. This 1 percent gives savers some return on their accounts (although precious little these days) and gives the bank enough—4 percent—to make a return on its capital and cover its costs. Everybody comes out ahead.

It is no different if a business, small or large, goes into the bank to borrow money to expand its manufacturing capacity or construct a residential building. Money from people who have deposited their cash at the bank is aggregated and provided to the business, which then pays interest that is divided between the depositors and the bank. (Of course, if the mortgage or business loan isn't paid back and the collateral behind the loan is insufficient, then the bank might have to be bailed out—as we all saw in 2008.) The amount of leverage in the borrower's business model and the amount of leverage in the bank's capital structure affect the risk in the deal and the magnitude of the returns—as we will discuss later. The process on either side of the equation—the aggregation of money from those who have it, and the distribution to those who need it—can get a whole lot more complex, of course. But at the end of the day, Wall Street's profits are keyed to its role as the access point for capital—both when it is pooled and when it is lent. In theory, if it pays less for money—what it pays depositors and others from whom it borrows money—than it receives from those to whom it lends (the difference is referred to as the spread), the bank should make money.

The transactions I just described involve somebody borrowing from the bank—assuming a debt obligation that has to be repaid. Those types of deals define the first general purpose that banks serve.

The other critical function of the capital markets is to serve as a place to raise equity for companies—such as the IPOs discussed in the analyst cases—and to ensure the liquidity of the markets where people who own that equity can trade. (This liquidity is what permits the ease and speed of the "exit" we talked about in the context of Hirschman's Exit Voice and Loyalty.) Better liquidity means people can sell their investments more readily for cash, and then trade the cash for stock positions in other companies. This is the process that ensures capital is allocated where market investors see the best returns.

There are, of course, many variables at play in this process of what the experts would call capital formation and capital allocation, variables relating to sometimes subtle differences between debt and equity, with differing degrees of risk, return, liquidity, and management say. All those variables are now woven together into an increasingly complex world.

But never forget: Wall Street is there to raise and allocate capital—both debt and equity—from those who have it to those who need it, and to render advice to clients who come in multiple shapes and sizes.

So how much money should Wall Street get for playing this role? Historically, folks on Wall Street did well, earning returns in the form of salaries and bonuses that competed with lawyers and doctors—but not *that* much more. Bankers were part of the "professional" class—but they didn't have gargantuan returns compared to others in that world. When the new emerging titans of the street broke the million-dollar barrier in the early '80s it sent shock waves through the market. A new era was dawning—and suddenly the ability to move money and keep a bigger and bigger piece of the upside transformed Wall Street. As the pie got bigger, the crumbs from the pie that intermediaries kept, to use Tom Wolfe's metaphor, also got bigger. When Michael Milken—subsequently sent to jail for insider trading—earned $500 million in 1987, it defined an entirely new era.

What seemed to transform Wall Street more than anything was a sequence of bubbles: Periods when asset valuations rose faster than normal, and in ways that in the end defied reason or logic. The frequency of bubbles that permitted these huge escalations in valuation—which in turn permitted the bankers to push the transactions that earned them the huge fees—was perhaps the defining phenomenon of the era. Of course, so were the deregulation that accompanied our misguided faith in self-regulation and the breakdown of fiduciary obligation discussed above. But to flesh out our understanding of Wall Street and the myths that attach to it, there are several critical features that must be understood—bubbles, conflicts of interest, leverage, and OPM.

GALBRAITH AND WOLFE:

TWO GENUINE MASTERS OF THE UNIVERSE

Let's begin by briefly digging into the wonderful historical analysis of John Kenneth Galbraith—one of the great economists and economic historians of recent times. His brilliant volume *A Short History of Financial Euphoria* captures more about the way financial markets generate bubbles and empower financiers than just about any other book I have read. We will also give a quick nod to the brilliance of Tom Wolfe, whose *Bonfire of the Vanities* captured the psyche of the "Masters of the Universe" who emerge whenever there appears to be a financial tide of success, however transitory.

As is so often the case, the best commentaries were written long ago but have an eerie capacity to be relevant and analytically correct with respect to what we live through much thereafter. So it is for Thucydides'

volume on the Peloponnesian wars, which continues to have metaphor-
ical application to all of subsequent history. And such is the case for Galbraith's *A Short History of Financial Euphoria*. The book is an essential
disquisition on the bubbles—and the fundamental truths of the capital markets that drive them—that have appeared with an inevitability
throughout modern capitalism.

Granted, the gap between Galbraith's book and the current era—he
first published *A Short History* in 1990, after the crash of 1987—is a bit
narrower than is the case for Thucydides' writing and the modern era.
But the amazing applicability of just about everything Galbraith wrote
to the cataclysm of 2008 is just as remarkable.

Galbraith sets out in the book to explain the inevitability of boom and
bust cycles in capitalism. In doing so he reveals critical lessons about
both markets and the psyche of the investors who drive those markets.
He observes—rightly—that no regulatory environment or genuine understanding of economics can save an institution when euphoria, or
what he calls mass insanity, takes over. Valuation of assets—the products being bought and sold, whether Dutch tulip bulbs or houses in
Arizona—is driven as much by emotion as hard mathematical analysis.
When a feeling of euphoria overtakes a market, doubters—those who
profess skepticism as the markets continue to be inflated by a generalized euphoria—will be challenged for a lack of confidence in markets
themselves, and it will be said that they doubt the inherent wisdom and
perfection of markets. Indeed, the doubters end up missing the massive
appreciation in wealth that accretes during the ride upwards! And so
during this entire period they are cast as Cassandras, and have a hard
time gaining credibility. The seeming inevitability of the continuing
rise in valuations permits those who proselytize a blind faith in the wisdom of markets to cast aspersions on those who doubt the validity of the
market. And in that environment, where each trade seems to produce
nothing but new riches, any call for greater regulatory action to forestall
trading or practices that appear to be distorting the market—such as a
requirement that borrowers actually have income sufficient to repay the
debt underlying the mortgage they are assuming—is seen as heresy.

As markets wind their way up this seemingly unending spiral of esca-
lating prices, new types of participants emerge: first, those who actually
believe in a "new paradigm" that permits prices to go in only one direction—up; and second, those who are more sophisticated and recognize
that a bubble has been inflated, but believe they will be able to time their
exit so that they can ride the upside without being harmed on the downside. The claim of a new paradigm for pricing is one of the sure pieces
of evidence that a bubble has emerged, and that the traditional—and
usually theoretically correct—valuation methods of the past are being
ignored to rationalize pricing that makes little sense.

When the bubble inevitably bursts, both groups flee—hoping to escape the crushing losses that result. Those who knew the downdraft was coming but felt they could time their departure to beat other market players are usually disappointed, becoming merely more fodder for the crash; those who had consumed the narcotic of belief in a new paradigm suddenly find their emotions dashed as well, and the logic of the "new paradigm" suddenly looks as thin as any Ponzi scheme. Whether Dutch tulip bulbs in 1637, or housing in 2008, the emotions and rationalizations are the same.

How does all this occur? As Galbraith observes, the euphoria that sweeps through the crowd converts many individual of reasonably good sense to the stupidity against which "the very Gods Themselves contend in vain." The speculative fever seems to destroy the intelligence of those involved. Indeed, recall the frequency with which many touted the creation of new paradigms over the past decades! First in the dot-com bubble, when companies with no revenue and no real prospect for revenue had market caps of billions of dollars, and then during the housing bubble, when bungalows sold for millions, "new paradigms" for valuation were claimed to have been created. Risk, it was said, has been eliminated through the wizardry of new vehicles and instruments, permitting the new paradigm to justify ever-escalating prices. Tech companies would figure out ways to "monetize" every small piece of data—even though there was no apparent party willing to pay. And credit default swaps eliminated risk, we were told. Risk had been apportioned among so many layers of debt and spread across so many mortgages that everybody was guaranteed to make money. If only it were so. Yet this language—reflective of every bubble in history—is the rationalization that soothes the mind of even more careful investors.

Critically important, Galbraith observes, is the scorn that is heaped upon doubters as the mania is in its early stages. All those who want to believe and who are profiting from the run-up in pricing dismiss the skeptics with the back of a hand. His historical examples include not only Paul Warburg in 1929 but also Galbraith himself in 1986. Speak ill of the wealth being created, the brilliance of the new breed of financiers who are profiting, and you are suddenly the subject of scorn. I can attest from my own experience that trying to stand in front of the rising tide of the market—even one that is no more than a bubble—is hardly possible. Just look at *The Wall Street Journal*'s unceasing rhetorical attack—echoed by many in the political world—on anybody who cast doubt on the way Wall Street was inflating any of the bubble's over the past 25 years.

As Galbraith observes, his effort to seek a rise in margin requirements—as a way of preventing wild speculation—even as far back as the 1950s set off anger and animus that he had rarely encountered, in any context. Increasing the margin requirement, the minimum amount of cash needed to complete many financial transactions, would have been akin to actually requiring purchasers of homes during the subprime bubble to make a meaningful down payment, or requiring banks that made home mortgages to keep those loans on their own balance sheets, reasonable and smart ways to prevent wild and misguided speculation. But as he observes: "The euphoric episode is protected and sustained by the will of those who are involved, in order to justify the circumstances that are making them rich. And it is equally protected by the will to ignore, exorcise, or condemn those who express doubts."

Galbraith focuses on two intellectual errors that contribute to speculative bubbles. First is the "extreme brevity of the financial memory.... There can be few fields of human endeavor in which history counts for so little as in the world of finance." I have often felt that the lessons we learn from financial disaster are akin to the lessons we learn as drivers after getting a speeding ticket. Without admitting too much, isn't it the case that for about 30 miles or so we stay within the speed limit, but begin thereafter the inevitable acceleration that caused the problem in the first place? The amnesia that attaches to what should be financial learning is similar and forces us to relive history over and over.

The second intellectual error is what Galbraith calls the "specious association of money and intelligence"—the general societal presumption that those with substantial accumulated wealth "must be associated with some special genius." This, he observes, is of course fallacious. The unfortunate secret is that the accretion of great wealth is as often associated with luck or timing as it is with actual wisdom. Steve Jobs is an exception, not the rule. Indeed, the subspecies of this flawed logic, which courses through our entire culture, is that "we compulsively associate unusual intelligence with the leadership of the great financial institutions—the large banking, investment banking, insurance, and brokerage houses." In practice, those who rose to those positions often got there because they were willing to accept the flawed reasoning that was driving the bubble in the first instance. Financial genius, he observes wryly, "is before the fall."

A wonderful recent example of the self-indulgence of those at the top of the financial world came from Jamie Dimon, the CEO of JPMorgan Chase. In answer to a question from an analyst that Dimon deemed not sufficiently intelligent, Dimon stated: "That's why I am richer than you are." The onslaught of regulatory issues and management failures now confronting JPMorgan Chase may make Dimon wish he had been a bit more circumspect in his observation.

Building on top of these psychological errors is another: the false sense that financial innovation can properly limit and minimize the risk attendant to the central feature common to every bubble—excess debt and leverage. Whether it is the evolution of the corporation with limits on liability, or junk bonds, or securitized debt, each of these "innovations" was ascribed the power to defuse the malignancy of excess debt, but each turned out to be little more than a placebo. As Galbraith states:

> "The rule is that financial operations do not lend themselves to innovation. What is recurrently so described and celebrated is, without exception, a small variation on an established design, one that owes its distinctive character to the brevity of the financial memory. The word of finance hails the invention of the wheel over and over again, often in a slightly more unstable version. All financial innovation involves, in one form or another, the creation of debt secured in greater or lesser adequacy by real assets."

And as we all know, when the assets that secure the debt are inadequate, and the inevitable burst occurs, a tidal wave of defaults and insolvency results. This excess debt with insufficient collateral, the excess ratio of debt to equity, is the narcotic that has doomed so many. And that narcotic is called leverage.

Leverage is the drug that has coursed through the bloodstream of every bubble and crisis. Just as a crack addict is unable to wean himself from the next hit, so too were borrowers and bankers addicted to the enormous financial highs that leverage could provide if properly timed. Yet the inevitable loss of judgment that attaches to ever-higher leverage ratios has made every so-called "innovation"—from junk bonds to LBOs to securitized debt—each merely another in a line of debt-related narcotics that produce addicts and a crash thereafter.

The final element that runs through the bubbles is that after each crash there is anger and recrimination, focused most aggressively on those who were most admired before—the leaders of the very financial institutions previously thought to be geniuses. The public seeks a lightning rod for the anger that has been generated. Calls for regulation are inevitable, but what will be ignored is the aberrant optimism that underlay the speculation in the first place. Indeed, we have seen this anger, mixed with an appropriate call for prosecution of true wrongdoing, drive much political rhetoric over the past several years.

As is well known, I have been a loud and consistent voice in favor of both more prosecutions and greater regulation. And I believe in each of those views deeply. Yet as Galbraith wisely points out, the surge of anger must also be recognized as a natural emotional response to the improper deference that was paid earlier to these same executives before the crash. Part of our desire to focus the anger on specific individuals is that as devotees of the free market we cannot accept that the market itself has been flawed. The market is neutral and accurate. As Galbraith says: "Markets in our culture are a totem; to them can be ascribed no inherent tendency or fault."

As a consequence, we want desperately to find individuals at fault—rather than the entire structure of the market. The arc of emotions that permits bubbles and euphoria to morph into anger and a demand for retribution has been followed multiple times. And it will be again.

Yet as has been clear from all that precedes and follows this chapter, it is sometimes the very structure of the market that we need to recognize as having been flawed. The behavior of individuals who were in a position uniquely to manage and affect the decisions made by the major entities that controlled capital must be criticized. But market structures themselves are often also to blame. Hence my effort in this volume to improve our understanding of how markets must be more clearly understood.

The second volume that captures these "bubble" moments—and supplements Galbraith—is Tom Wolfe's brilliant *Bonfire of the Vanities*. The characters in *Bonfire* capture the intersecting worlds that get caught up in market turmoil and crashes. The phrase "Masters of the Universe," applied to the Wall Street plutocracy, as with so many other turns of phrase that Wolfe has bequeathed to us, sums up an entire epoch. The Wall Street financier driving a sports car with the world at his feet—yet ultimately just as vulnerable and devoid of substance as the synthetic market products they trade—is the beauty of Wolfe's image. The lives of the Masters of the Universe are no more real than the equity that was supposed to underlie the deals that were financed by the securitized debt that disappeared. The evanescent nature of the ascent of the Masters is akin to the very bubbles they inflated. Yet because of the psychological flaw that Galbraith identified and that we all play into, confusing great wealth with great intellectual acumen, the Masters of the Universe continue to get away with it—until the havoc of the market crash does its damage.

The diagnostics of Galbraith and the metaphors of Wolfe capture so much of what one needs to know about the inner psyche of Wall Street. If we all brought the skepticism they teach to our behavior as bubbles are being inflated, we would save ourselves much harm. But we haven't done so in the past; and we are unlikely to do so in the future.

CONFLICTS OF INTEREST DO NOT

EQUAL SYNERGIES

Let's weave together a few of the strands from prior chapters: Repeal of the New Deal-era regulatory framework permitted creation of behemoth banking entities where structural flaws necessarily emerged.

And despite Jack Grubman's devout desire, these conflicts did not of their own accord morph into synergies. The structural flaws on Wall Street created enormous and irreconcilable conflicts. The stress applied to the fundamental agency relationships that undergird the proper functioning of our major financial companies—those between analysts and investors, insurance brokers and clients for instance—have led to enormous violations of fiduciary duty that have unwound the core ethics of Wall Street. These conflicts are now so deeply rooted in the foundations of Wall Street that sequential crises were inevitable as the integrity of advice rendered was debased over time. The spectacle of Goldman executives attempting to justify their betting against the own clients, in hearings conducted by senator Carl Levin over the Abacus transaction, is symptomatic of the warped logic that overtook the street. Part of the problem might be that in the conflicted world in which too many senior bankers live, they can't even define who their client is!

OPINION LETTERS FOR SALE

Let me add two more examples of the sorts of conflicts of interest that have permeated the street. The first is symptomatic of the era in which CEOs are told only what they want to hear. It was written about persuasively by none other than Don Kempf—the former general counsel of Morgan Stanley. Kempf is the hardnosed but extraordinarily smart fellow with whom we negotiated parts of the analyst global settlement and who was responsible for drafting the "Spitzer amendments"—proposed and supported by members of the House Financial Services Committee at the behest of Wall Street and designed to divest the New York State Attorney General's office of jurisdiction to do our most important cases. (The SEC, parenthetically, supported these amendments, in another show of spinelessness. Many of my battles with the SEC were triggered by their willingness to support jurisdiction-stripping amendments, which they knew to be bad law and bad for enforcement.)

Don highlighted the conflicts of interest inherent in the way "opinion letters" are produced. These letters are provided by the groups I identified as facilitator—lawyers, accountants, investment bankers—to justify the actions to be taken by a particular company. They are ordinarily written to the board, and opine for instance on the valuation of a takeover target—and hence the adequacy of a price offered to shareholders—or the rectitude of an accounting procedure, even when it might be suspect. Lehman Brothers got a major international law firm to bless—in an opinion letter—the insane Repo 105 transactions that essentially permitted the illusory disappearance of over $50 billion in debt from Lehman's books. The debt became all too real in short order.

The amazing thing about these opinion letters is that they almost always say exactly what the board WANTS to hear. And why is that? Because providing the opinion is merely one of many aspects of the work done for the board or client company by the firm or entity providing the opinion. And it knows darn well that if it doesn't come to the right conclusion about the opinion it has been asked to reach, it may well lose the rest of the work—and the fees from the transaction it is working on. Here is what Don said, writing from the belly of the beast: "Regulators, academics, and others have been particularly critical of the practice of directors relying solely on the investment bankers involved in the transaction at issue to provide fairness opinions. The primary reason for this is the potential conflict of interest that arises from having an investment bank whose compensation is contingent on the completion of the transaction opining on whether or not the transaction should be completed. Stated differently, the bank will not be paid if it cannot find fairness." Even though Don suggests that a new paradigm should emerge with independent opinions being proffered, the range and enormity of conflicts that pervade the provision of opinion letters, usually still by related parties with a boilerplate statement of disclosure, makes these letters close to meaningless. They are useful as an insurance policy for board members to point to, but not really as an independent judgment of value or propriety for any of the other parties to the transaction. They are usually as worthless as the ratings issued by S&P or Moody's. It should be no mystery that opinion letter are essentially bought from the range of "facilitators" who surround CEOs.

Another example of such conflicted advice, of course, was in the Grasso compensation case, discussed in detail above, where Mercer was totally conflicted.

THE NY FED: A SWAMP OF CONFLICTS

If you want another window into how conflicts of interest have destroyed the integrity of the governance of our banking system, look at the NY Fed. Now understand that the NY Fed—perhaps the single most powerful regulatory body you know nothing about—is actually owned by the banks. And its board membership reflects that: Take a look at a list of some of its board members from 2005–08, as the crisis was building, and as the NY Fed sat there doing virtually nothing to challenge the high leverage game of bubble inflation we were playing: Sandy Weill, chair of Citibank; Dick Fuld, chair of Lehman Brothers; Jeff Immelt, chair of GE, which includes GE Capital, one of the biggest commercial lenders in the nation; Jamie Dimon, chair of JPMorgan Chase; and Stephen Friedman, chair of Stony Point Capital, but more importantly the former chair of Goldman Sachs.

And this is the body that had and has the power to determine whether banks—the banks that created the crisis of 2008—are managing their leverage ratios properly? You don't think this simply cries out for unraveling the conflicts inherent in having the fox guarding the hen house?

Recall, Tim Geithner was president of the NY Fed from 2003 until 2009, when he became Treasury Secretary. He was in the single most pivotal position to alter the mania for leverage and uncontrolled lending and securitization that created the crisis of 2008. Yet he did little or nothing to confront this obvious problem, for all the reasons Galbraith articulated.

Who, by the way, chose Geithner to be president of the NY Fed? A committee whose membership included Hank Greenberg of AIG and John Whitehead of Goldman. The NY Fed is one of the quintessential failed institutions—totally dominated by the very entities it is supposed to regulate, emotionally subservient to their needs, and ultimately without teeth in negotiating the terms of the loans it made during the crisis to banks that needed capital infusions. (To see more about the serious questions—never properly investigated, relating to the NY Fed and the bailout of AIG, see my *Slate* articles on that subject.)

One of many examples of the inherent conflicts baked into the NY Fed governance structure emerged when the Fed guaranteed all commercial paper in the marketplace. This guarantee got little attention compared to the cash infusions that were occurring at the time—and even less attention was focused on the fact that the single largest beneficiary of the guarantee was GE. GE Capital would have been unable to finance its cash needs without this guarantee, and it would have in all probability led to GE's bankruptcy. Yet who was on the board of the NY Fed at the time this guarantee was extended: the chairman of GE: Jeff Immelt. We know nothing of the contact between the NY Fed and GE at the time the guarantee was being discussed or negotiated, and while there is no reason to think anything improper was done, the fact of so many direct conflicts between the governance of the entity and the benefits that flowed is deeply problematic.

To make it worse, and perhaps turn tragedy into farce—Immelt was on the board not as an industry representative but as a public representative! How ludicrous is that? It is as foolish as the failed effort by the NYSE to put Sandy Weill on the board as a public representative. It demonstrates just how insular and unknowing these boards had become.

This is just one example of the interlocking interests—the inherent conflict that was at the very top of the NY Fed.

S & P: ANALYSTS ALL OVER AGAIN

If you want a more recent case demonstrating that the issue of conflicts of interest continue as they have in the past, take a look at the case against the rating agency Standard & Poor's, filed by the Department of Justice on February 4, 2013. Of course, this case was brought five years later than it should have been, but it sets out the identical structural tension we confronted in the analyst cases: that between integrity in the critique of risk versus the desire to appease those who really pay the bills. In the case of the rating agencies, the bills were being paid and the profits assured by the very companies whose debt was being rated! Just as the analysts were giving guaranteed "Buy" ratings on stocks where the IPO was the real financial reward for the investment banks, so here the rating agency was giving inflated ratings for fear of losing as clients the underwriters of debt who paid the bills. Integrity was sacrificed for market share and revenue. And who lost? The entire economy collapsed because the ratings proved false, and AAA debt proved as worthless as the scraps of paper the ratings were printed on. The complaint is worth reading.

Just to amuse you—and to show that the structural issue of conflicts goes way beyond the financial sector, here is a quick story about rankings of another sort. Back in the mid-1990s I got a call from a friend who asked if I wanted to represent a boxer who intended to sue Don King—the mega-boxing promoter. That should be fun, I thought. Here is what it was all about: William Guthrie, a/k/a Kid Chocolate, was ranked Number One in the light heavyweight division, and so according to the rules of each of the three ranking bodies was to be guaranteed a shot at the title. But that all changed when Guthrie decided he didn't want Don King to be his promoter any more. Because Guthrie felt King was not treating him fairly, was not giving him a sufficient piece of the prize money, Guthrie sought a new promoter. Suddenly, because King in truth controlled the ranking agencies, Guthrie's ranking fell, and he was denied his title fight. He was blackballed by the boxing ranking entities because he wanted to drop Don King as his promoter. The integrity of the boxing ratings had been subverted and made totally subservient to the financial needs of the promoters. So we went to court—state and federal—sued King and the ranking bodies, and got a court order requiring that they give Guthrie his fight! This led to perhaps one of my great moments as a lawyer: In the ring after winning his title fight, and having been crowned the light heavyweight champion of the world, Guthrie was asked how it felt. And he said: "I want to thank three people: God, my trainer, and my lawyer Eliot Spitzer." Clients never say thank you! And he had done so on live, national TV.

Later, when I was Attorney General, I was chair of the AG task force on boxing, and we sought to create an independent ranking entity—separate from those with a financial interest in the bouts. At the end of the day, it didn't matter whether it was stock analysts, bond rating agencies, or boxing—conflicts are conflicts and they debase the integrity of the product.

                              * * *

So here is the logic thus far in this chapter:

If you accept that Galbraith's critique is correct, that a euphoric emotion drives an "irrational exuberance" about markets, often rejecting saner calls for moderation or oversight, and then add on top of that the hubris brilliantly described by Wolfe, the conflicts inherent in the business models we have generated over the past years, and a near total absence of regulatory oversight, what emerges is a volatile and dangerous dynamic.

We will now add two dangerous accelerants: OPM and leverage.

OTHER PEOPLE'S MONEY

OPM are the most important letters in the alphabet to Wall Street: They stand for Other People's Money. That is what Wall Street titans play with. That is what they put at risk. That is what is lost when things go bad—not their own money. Now there is nothing necessarily wrong with the banks, mutual funds, pension fund managers, and others using the money of other folks as the pool of capital that they invest and trade. Indeed, that is what they are paid to do. But as we discussed above, where there is an agency relationship, where these folks are acting on behalf of others, the immediate question is: Are they acting in the interest of their clients—their fiduciaries—or somehow taking advantage of the relationship to pad their own pockets through an accretion of fees that result whether or not investments are well handled? More invidiously, you can see this as part of the process whereby banks keep the upside, through fee generation, and then lay off the downside risk—what we have come to call "socializing risk and privatizing gain." The perverse impact of incentives created by playing with OPM is at the root of many of the problems on Wall Street. As we saw with analysts, mutual fund fees, the trading patterns of many accounts, and the securitization of bad mortgages, when Wall Street can push the risk elsewhere yet keep the upside of fees, dangerous things result.

When you are playing with somebody else's money, you are willing to take greater risk—gamble bigger—be cavalier in a way that would simply not be possible if your own money, your kid's college education, were on the line. The upside—the bonuses and the carried interests that the Wall Street traders will receive—go up when the returns are big. Yet the traders do not shoulder the losses, creating the asymmetry in risk that creates pressure once again for improper risk taking.

Here are two examples of how OPM comes into play.

At one level the entire subprime cataclysm was a consequence of the perverse incentives resulting from OPM. Realize that—as we discussed in Chapter Two above—virtually all of the bad debt was securitized, meaning sold to others in complex debt instruments that pulled together many mortgages into "bundled" obligations. The theory was that the bundling diminished the risk. But more central to the incentives was that the fees from issuing, selling, processing, and refinancing were the economic drivers—not the prospect of receiving interest and then principal on the underlying obligation. The downside risk of default was shifted to those who bought the securitized debt. The incentive as a result was to issue as great a volume of loans as possible, since the risk of declining quality did not reside with the issuer. Others bore the risk, and the issuers retained the steady stream of fees. If banks had needed to hold the mortgages—and put their own capital at risk—they would have acted differently.

And second, do not forget, the greatest demonstration of the risk-shifting and consequence of OPM was the bailout—not just TARP, but the $7 trillion in loans and guarantees offered to financial entities to overcome their liquidity problems. The financial entities took the risk, kept the upside in fees, bonuses, profit sharing, and then got public money to cover the downside. And this subsidy continues, in the form of a massive guarantee—calculated to be worth $83 billion per year by none other than Bloomberg media. Virtually the entire profits of the financial sector come from their ability to tap into "OPM" for guarantees, capital, and risk-shifting.

LEVERAGE

If OPM is the first accelerant, the second is leverage. As Galbraith explained, leverage is a narcotic. Let me give you some numerical examples to demonstrate how leverage can "juice" returns on the upside—while also creating enormous exposure if things don't go quite as planned.

Imagine the following simplified real estate deal: You purchased a 200,000 rentable square foot residential building for $100 million—or $500 a square foot—with the following capital structure:

> $5 million—equity
> $95 million—debt at 7% interest only
> $100 million total investment

Now imagine the following costs and revenues:

> Interest cost: $6.65 million ($95 million @ 7% interest only)
> Labor $1.0 million
> Real estate taxes: $1.5 million
> Other soft costs: $0.5 million
> Total costs: $9.65 million
> Revenue: $11 million ($55 per square foot annual rent)

The profit equals $1.35 million—a return on equity of 27 percent. That is extraordinarily healthy, especially when combined with the other tax advantages that result from real estate, such as depreciation.

But recognize how thin the margins are: If interest jumps merely to 9 percent after three years, then interest costs leap to $8.55 million—a net increase of $1.9 million—overwhelming any profit. Sound familiar? When adjustable rates were reset, suddenly even those leveraged deals that pretended to make sense from a cash flow perspective became cash flow negative.

Or imagine that rent drops from $55 per square foot to $48 per square foot—a not-unheard of reality. Revenue then drops to $9.6 million, making the building a loser even with the original interest rate.

The point is obvious: Leverage created great returns when things were perfect, but also created margins that were so thin that the possibility of tipping into negative territory was all too real—as we all saw.

Now imagine a different capital structure: If instead of $95 million in debt, the building had been purchased with a more prudent debt of $60 million, interest costs would be $4.2 million, increasing profit to $3.8 million on invested capital of $40 million, a return of 9.5 percent—not the 27 percent garnered with more leverage. But look at the comfort created in terms of lost cash flow. Even if interest were to jump to 9 percent, as we discussed above, then the building would still be profitable—with a net of $2.6 million, a return of 6.5 percent.

Leverage can juice returns, but eliminate virtually all margin of error. We all saw that after 2008.

Now switch briefly into the zone of bank finance. The lack of bank capital—the analog to a lack of equity in real estate—can be equally dangerous. When banks fund their loan portfolio with 3 percent capital and 97 percent from borrowed sources, then if only 3 percent of the loan portfolio goes bad, the bank can go under!

As we all know, when things soured in 2008, we lost a lot more than that, and the capital margins the banks had proved woefully inadequate.

As you have seen, when leverage ratios are outside the bounds of conservative investing, and values fall even a small bit, then companies are technically thrown into a state of insolvency, and the value of all equity goes to zero. Moreover, when companies are capitalized with significant leverage, and depend upon daily borrowing to maintain their ongoing businesses, as Lehman and others were doing just before the crisis of 2008, then the market can quickly turn against such a company, as fear of failure eliminates the ability to borrow even short term. Such a credit crisis is exactly what undid the financial houses in 2008. Managers and regulators of even minimal competence would never have permitted the leverage ratios of these entities to come close to where they were before the crash. Again, this wanton disregard for the realities of the market on the part of those supposedly schooled in evaluating risk should make us wary of again relying upon these same folks. The story that emerged proves Galbraith's point about the unreality of analysis that pervades the market when a bubble is inflated.

***

This brief chapter has given you—I hope—a rough understanding of the psyche and some of the dynamics on Wall Street that contributed to the cataclysm of '08. It is not as complicated as they want you to think it is. Behind their story of complexity are a couple of simple principles: Conflicts of interest lead to violations of fiduciary duty; no amount of financial alchemy can turn excess debt into a riskless investment; leverage is a narcotic; financial wizards are wise only when the market is rising; bubbles are emotional moments where all rational analysis has been lost; playing with OPM lets Wall Street take our risk and turn it into their profit; and somehow, we always end up paying the bill at the end of the day.

7

HARD-TO-SANCTION
CORPORATIONS

Rule Seven:

Corporations always seem

to get off scot-free.

One of my favorite signs of recent years was raised by the folks at Occupy Wall Street: "We will know corporations are people when Texas executes one." The sign is sardonic, but makes a powerful point. Corporations have demanded—and been given—many of the rights of individuals; yet sanctioning them as effectively as sanctioning individuals has proven awfully difficult. Corporations revel in the rights of personhood—just consider Citizens United and its aftermath. But corporations have few if any of the responsibilities and potential exposure to sanctions that come with real personhood. This tension—both real and perceived—has led to the enormous frustration that manifests itself in our political conversations.

Start with the simplest question: What does it mean to hold a corporation responsible for wrongdoing? Who should be held accountable? The board? Senior management? The shareholders? Only the individual or individuals who had actual knowledge and/or participated in the wrongdoing, thereby often precluding the possibility of broader liability? What about the most senior executives who created the environment and incentives that generated the wrongdoing—even if they were not involved directly themselves? This problem has confounded even well-meaning prosecutors. And too often it has permitted spineless prosecutors to let egregious wrongdoing go unpunished.

This problem is at the root of amazing—and legitimate—public dissatisfaction with our judicial system. After all this time, not a single major financial firm has been indicted, nor has a single senior Wall Street executive gone to jail for the massive misrepresentations that caused the cataclysm of 2008. Yet we send small-time thieves away for decades.

And the Department of Justice spent vast resources failing to convict Roger Clemens of using steroids—or lying to Congress—and failed even to find the evidence relating to Lance Armstrong. Is this really what DOJ thought our prosecutorial priorities should be? Justice seems to be a rare commodity in the arena of our largest frauds. Accountability has been totally absent.

Start with the necessary first question: When we sanction wrongdoing, what are we trying to accomplish? There is the goal of *specific deterrence*: stopping the individual actor who did something wrong this time from doing it again; the goal of *general deterrence*: stopping those not involved in the particular activity at hand from acting badly in the future because they see that if they do something wrong, bad stuff happens to them or their institution; the goal of *restitution* to those injured: making them whole for the loss they suffered; the goal of societal *articulation of moral outrage* or at least definition of boundaries for acceptable behavior; and the goal of *injunctive relief*: either affirmative by requiring that people *do* something, or negative by requiring that they *not do* something, thus changing the circumstances that led to the improper behavior in the first place. That is a whole lot of social engineering to accomplish in each case! Which explains why reaching all those objectives in the complex dynamic of a corporate prosecution is difficult.

When you look at the recidivism rate of corporate wrongdoing—the same actors doing bad things over and over—the failure to get money back to a lot of people who were damaged by the financial crisis and other major frauds, and the lack of remorse that seems to be shown by the financial sector as a whole, it is hard not to conclude that we are failing to accomplish a whole lot through our judicial system right now.

Our crisis of corporate law enforcement doesn't relate just to failing to prove the wrongdoing. That can sometimes be pretty easy, as the lengthy litany of recent cases establishes: lying about the value of mortgages, money laundering, throwing bad ratings on junk debt, proffering knowingly bad advice, discrimination in marketing of securitized mortgages, bid rigging in so many sectors—from LIBOR to pharmaceuticals. The list keeps going. And this has not been an unusual stretch.

The crisis is that we have been doing virtually nothing to accomplish the remedial objectives we defined for our judicial system even once the nature of the wrongdoing itself is clear and provable. Consequently, few people think the outcomes have been "just" at any deeper level. It is a crisis of remedies as much as a crisis of proof.

Contrast the corporate context with our ordinary "street crime" dynamic. When somebody—a real person—commits a violent crime, it is not so tough to understand how sanctions should be imposed. Somebody who robs or steals can be sent to jail. This accomplishes specific and general deterrence. Restitution as a concept is easy to grasp, if the criminal has any assets to use as a source of repayment. But the complexity of the large-scale frauds committed by institutions—not individuals—makes these sanctioning decisions more complicated.

In thinking about the choices made by prosecutors with respect to corporate acts—how to charge and what remedies to seek—it is important to realize that many of the cases we discuss *could* have been brought as criminal cases against the corporations themselves. Here is why: Under our criminal law theory, the actions of individuals sufficiently high in the corporation can bind the corporation and can be attributable to the corporation for purposes of criminal liability. So in theory the director of research at Merrill who knew of or countenanced the knowing proffering of bad advice, or the senior directors at HSBC who saw and tolerated structured money laundering, or the senior officers at the many banks who knew of and participated in fixing the LIBOR rate could have had their criminal behavior held against the entire company. This could have led to the indictment of the entire company. Yet despite this, no criminal cases have been brought against the companies.

Would criminal cases have been appropriate? When the entities have had prior and repetitive violations of law, I think the answer is unambiguously yes.

But before jumping to this conclusion, how do we deal with the argument made most recently by U.S. Attorney General Eric Holder and others about the risk of collateral consequences if criminal cases are brought against major companies? He was unfortunately honest in his observation that he was unwilling to prosecute many of the largest institutions because of these collateral consequences. Holder's statement, echoed by Lanny Breuer, formerly head of the Justice Department's criminal division, explains their woeful timidity in this regard.

Holder said: "I am concerned that the size of some of these institutions becomes so large that it does become difficult for us to prosecute them when we are hit with indications that if you do prosecute, if you do bring a criminal charge, it will have a negative impact on the national economy, perhaps even the world economy. And I think that is a function of the fact that some of these institutions have become too large."

The administration did not, of course, do anything to limit or diminish the size of these institutions. Indeed, they have only grown since the crisis of 2008. The administration placed handcuffs on itself by failing to address the problem of scale in our financial services sector.

Thinking about Holder's statement makes us realize that "too big to fail" has officially become "too big to jail" and even "too big to prosecute." Holder's statement also raises the necessary question: Who has been giving DOJ the information or advice upon which to make the "economic impact" decisions? It would be a fertile area of inquiry to seek all communications between Justice and any governmental or nongovernmental entity about the economic impact of any prosecution. Because whoever is rendering this advice—something Justice is not competent to determine on its own—has acquired veto power over our prosecutorial decisions. In effect has the Treasury Department been exercising veto power over DOJ prosecutorial decisions—creating a virtual zone of immunity for our largest companies?

But that issue aside, what are the consequences Holder is so worried about? In some cases, a criminal conviction against a corporation would preclude the corporation's continuing to operate—resulting in a so-called "corporate death penalty." This is because various statutes deny licenses to companies that have committed felonies, so a felony would be an immediate bar to continued operation. And as Holder observed, this could have an impact on the economy—global or local—and many innocent people who worked for the company.

Yet in my view the collateral damage is vastly overstated; almost all entities have the capacity to regenerate—even if under a new name, with new ownership and new leadership—and forcing them to do so will have the deterrent effect we desire. And most companies would have no trouble continuing in operation once charged. They might suffer reputational harm, perhaps lose contracts, have certain loans be declared to be in default, and lose some personnel and public support. But that would probably be the proper price to be paid in the context of the violations of law they committed!

If, once HSBC agreed to a $1.92 billion fine to settle money-laundering charges, it had been forced to change leadership and ownership, and transfer its deposits to another entity and its investment banking relationships to a new bank, no enormous harm would have been done and the proper message would have been sent to banks that were only too happy to be recidivist money launderers. Most of the assets of companies like this can in fact be transferred if necessary: The skills and relationships of the people at the organization, whether bankers, accountants, lawyers, or computer wizards, do not disappear. And the hard assets clearly can be acquired and transferred.

Prosecutors wrongly look at the Lehman bankruptcy and use that as evidence of what might happen if a major entity were indicted. It is the wrong metaphor. Lehman's bankruptcy was the trigger for a massive economic debacle because there were systemic issues that had been ignored and Lehman's "interconnectedness" made it a fuse that then ignited a much larger crisis. Going forward, simply isolating one financial entity and unwinding its relationships can be done without causing the structural insecurity that Lehman's bankruptcy played into. And in the non-financial sector, the issues and scope of potential collateral harm are much more readily cabined.

So take as Conclusion One from this chapter that companies can and should be charged more often. "Charge them!" should be the rallying cry of those who want justice. Fear not the myth of "collateral damage."

Having said that, we should also acknowledge that figuring out how to charge and how to impose sanctions on large corporations is not easy. The cases I brought—some discussed earlier—from the prosecutions, guilty pleas, and civil remedies with the Gambinos; in the analyst cases, insurance and mutual fund cases—along with many others not discussed here—reveal that I too have struggled to find ways to solve this problem.

Let me take a short detour here to discuss the possibility of criminal cases and hence the prospect of jail time against the most senior executives at major financial service companies: If the cases can be made, they should be. But here prosecutors are usually being truthful—it is often not possible to prove "intent" against the most senior employees of the company. Consequently, criminal cases are often limited to mid-level employees. The problem is that showing the requisite level of knowledge, participation or intent on the part of those at the top can be difficult. Take the analysts cases: The analysts who misled might have been provably guilty of fraud. They made, we argued, knowing misrepresentations; but proving that senior executives knew the specific analyst's claims about the merit of particular stocks were knowingly wrong would have been virtually impossible. This "knowing" element is central to our sense of justice. And it should be. Remember: Being wrong about a stock recommendation is not a crime—being knowingly misleading is. The emails that were so probative about analyst misrepresentations simply didn't exist with respect to senior executives. And making a criminal case against the senior executives by proving the more creative theory of "willfully" disregarding the truth would have been a stretch, to say the least. A similar problem exists in other areas and fact patterns as well.[9]

A consequence of the inability to make a criminal case against the senior executives is that juries often think it unfair when only mid-level employees are subject to criminal sanctions. (I experienced firsthand the difficulty of prosecuting a mid-level employee whom the jury feels is being made a scapegoat for an entire business. "Jury nullification" will often lead to an acquittal on the theory that the "little guy" should not be held accountable when the big fish get away. This is an understandable emotion.)

So the obvious second conclusion of this chapter: If possible, charge senior executives, but realize that when that is not possible, mid-level employees appear sympathetic to a jury that believes they are taking the heat for those above them. But an extension of this reality is that if senior executives may be hard to charge individually, it becomes that much more important to hold the corporation as an entity legally responsible.

So let's run through the traditional sanctions, as applied against companies, and it will be evident why we often feel they are grotesquely inadequate. And realize that the remedies available for a corporate entity are pretty much the same in the criminal and civil context. Then let's see if there are some additional steps that might be taken.

What are the traditional sanctions: first, jail time; second, money, in the form of fines, penalties, and restitution; and third, injunctive relief—an order to stop doing something, or alternatively to start doing something. There are also a raft of other "softer" remedies—probation, monitorships, momentary loss of lines of business, that are a bit less significant in my view.

First: jail time. Let's face it, you can't really put a company in jail.

The second remedy: money. Here the problem is twofold: First, the amount, even if looks big on paper, is ordinarily not sufficient to have a major impact on a big organization. The HSBC fine of $1.92 billion was not a major hit to this global bank. The $1.4 billion in the analyst cases was similarly not really enough to send a significant message to the entities involved. In addition, the fines often are not even great enough to exact a penalty bigger than the profits earned by the entire scope of the illegal behavior, when one includes behavior not prosecuted. The fine is then seen as nothing more than a toll, a cost of doing business. This is especially the case when the company, in the civil context, has not had to admit wrongdoing. (More on that below.) Of course, the upside to money damages is that they can provide restitution to injured parties. While that was the virtue to the money in the analyst cases, the amount otherwise, I have to admit, was not enough to change behavior prospectively or genuinely impose a meaningful sanction.

And that is because of the second major issue with money damages: Who actually pays? Except in the unusual case where individuals are required to give up salary or a bonus, usually through clawbacks of some form, it is the shareholder who pays. Certainly if the amounts are big enough to be meaningful, only the shareholder—meaning the corporate treasury—can provide the needed resources. Now in theory shareholders will then apply pressure to management to avoid being sanctioned again, and that might provide some general deterrent effect. Yet the pain of this is too diffuse to be effective; the dollars rarely make any significant dent in shareholder equity, and the mechanisms of shareholder control are way too weak to lead shareholders to take action after sanctions are applied. Think about this in the context of the discussion in Chapter Five about corporate governance and *Exit, Voice, and Loyalty.*

Money damages are thus too often just factored into the cost of doing business, and are unlikely to alter behavior going forward, or really affect the way the bad actors look at what they have done. The proof of this is in the historical record. The unfortunate reality is that all the fines assessed against Wall Street and even the major environmental violators—from BP to Exxon—have hardly changed behavior or done more than put a tiny dent in one quarter's financial returns. The cavalier attitude of CEOs and senior management to paying fines should make it clear that fines alone do not alter corporate behavior. Just look at JPMorgan Chase's claim—and the public acceptance of the fact—that it has had great management under Jamie Dimon, even after the "London whale" episode, and even after it has paid $8.5 *billion* in fines and penalties since 2009, according to *JPMorgan Chase: Out of Control,* a report by Josh Rosner of Graham Fisher. That is a staggering amount, yet there seems not to have been any significant impact on JPMorgan management itself. A few folks were fired, top management continued in place, and the board even refused to support a shareholder resolution to separate the positions of chair and CEO.

But if jail doesn't have any meaning as a sanction against the company itself, and if money doesn't usually do enough, it is in the third arena that we have a real opportunity: injunctive relief. It is in this area that we tried to be creative when I was Attorney General. We tried to leverage the opportunity presented by the array of remedies and negotiating opportunities we had to figure out what structure had bred the improper behavior and then require that structural changes be put in place to address them head on. In that regard, how we thought about the injunctive opportunities in remedies, and sought to impose them, was fundamentally different.

Let me quickly walk through a few of our cases—some discussed earlier in this volume—but now just in the context of the remedies we sought to impose. Keep in mind, not all of them worked. But the idea of using creative injunctive relief to remedy structural issues and violations is the key. Then let me also suggest a few other ideas that we should include in our tool box of corporate sanctions.

Marsh Mac: back in Chapter One I discussed their old-fashioned bid rigging and price fixing scheme. The problem with Marsh and remedies began with their CEO. In a quite remarkable meeting in my office with the CEO, Jeff Greenberg, and his attorney, Greenberg refused even to acknowledge that the system of false bids, kickbacks, and market allocation was violative of the law. Any first-year law student would have diagnosed their behavior—as well as that of their co-conspirators, AIG and other major insurance carriers—as textbook criminal antitrust behavior. Greenberg's refusal to recognize reality here led to Step One: When I announced the criminal and civil cases, but only civil against the company itself, I also announced that I could not negotiate a resolution with the company as long as Greenberg was retained as the CEO. Many folks were startled. He was not individually liable because we could not establish evidence to place him squarely in the conduct at issue. But how foolish would it be to resolve a case with a CEO who didn't even recognize the impropriety of the behavior?

Did I effectively demand and get the CEO of Marsh Mac fired? I suppose so. It was not only the correct thing to do; it should be standard practice where the CEO has helped foster a culture of wrongdoing, failed to confront it head on, or turned a blind eye to it. This is so even if the CEO had no direct role in the specific behavior at issue. CEO departures in the midst of structural misbehavior should be much more common—indeed perhaps even obligatory. More on that below. Even if not directly involved, a management that fails to detect and alter structural misbehavior has clearly failed, and hence should be replaced. It should go without saying that only by creating a very different set of management incentives—such as the reality that forced departure follows from misbehavior within the company—can we effectively change behavior prospectively. So Lesson One from our Marsh case: Where structural wrongdoing has occurred and been undetected or accepted under the watch of a CEO, the CEO must go. Any CEO who remains must commit to a fundamental restructuring of the incentives and business model that gave rise to the problem. Otherwise there will never be true accountability.

Second, and at least as important, we got major insurers to agree to end the practice that was at the root of the incentive structure that had led to the corruption: contingent commissions that bred a fundamental violation of fiduciary duty and the law. Although this injunctive piece did not survive subsequent laxness from insurance regulators, it should have.

Recognizing that beyond the standard civil and criminal sanctions we needed to force a change in leadership at the company and then force a change in the very structure of the way the insurance products were sold is what was fundamentally different about the way we handled that case.

Akin to the remedy we sought in Marsh Mac was what we tried to do in the analyst cases. As discussed above, we strove for structural reform. Eliminating the conflicts of interest inherent in the business model was the objective. The global deal, heralded as one of the most significant reforms on Wall Street in years, might at the end of the day be judged a success or failure. But one thing we unquestionably succeeded in doing was highlighting for the world—and most importantly for consumers of Wall Street research—the inherent unreliability and conflict in the research that was issued by the major firms. Charles Schwab tried to capitalize on this during the height of the coverage of the scandal by running an ad mocking the advice provided by the major Wall Street firms, showing a pig, with the old cliché that you can't put lipstick on a pig.

The reforms we mandated were structural and surely controversial, but they were designed to go beyond merely placing a Band-Aid over the wound when the hemorrhaging continued below. Among the most important was that we required that consumers be provided genuinely "independent" research. Using the possibility of imposing civil and criminal penalties against the major firms as the negotiating lever to obtain this injunctive relief was deeply resented by the firms—but it was clearly the thing to do. We saw the corrosive impact of the conflicted research throughout the market, and hoped the structural reform we imposed would get the firms to be more loyal to the fiduciary duty that was supposed to guide their behavior. Unfortunately, as we saw when the subprime debt crisis exploded several years later, these same firms had not learned the lesson. But our message and mission were clear— no more standard, traditional remedies.

Looking back from the perspective of the past decade, I could in fact have been more demanding. I could have required that senior executives overseeing the major research divisions and perhaps the CEOs of the parent companies as well be forced to resign as part of the global settlement. They had created the policies and corrupt incentives that led to the corrosive behavior. Without their departure there was not enough accountability and hence deterrence built into the remedy we imposed.

In a totally different context and sector—big pharma—we tried the same approach of seeking major injunctive relief, not just money. In our litigation with GlaxoSmithKline, at issue were misrepresentations by the company about the impact of Paxil on teenagers, and the marketing of Paxil for off-label purposes. Yet the root of the problem was the lack of transparency with respect to pharmaceutical testing. As I discussed, we required Glaxo to create a database with vastly additional disclosure about the testing results from its clinical testing regimes. A simple fine would have been inconsequential. The tectonic shift in pharma data testing release we sought has contributed to a newfound level of accountability in big pharma's claims with respect to the drugs they create. That is, after all, the objective.

The mutual funds cases present another example of creative sanctions designed to get at the root systemic issue, not just the top tier most-visible violation. Recall, the proximate violation of fiduciary duty was the late trading that benefited some fund clients to the detriment of others. For a significant fee, essentially a bribe, the mutual fund companies were transferring substantial profits from one group of clients— who were owed a fiduciary duty—to another set of clients—who had paid extra.

But the real scandal was mutual funds fees and the way fees were set. Interlocking boards were routinely awarding themselves fees higher than appropriate. This violation was costing investors billions of dollars every year.

So we insisted that fees be cut. Why? This was the only way to address the root violation of fiduciary duty. The SEC refused to go along. *The Wall Street Journal* editorial board howled. In the end our settlements resulted in fee reductions totaling billions of dollars retrospectively and much more than that prospectively. Even Judge Posner, the intellectual leader of free market ideology, agreed with us. (See "Judge Posner Wrote What?" in *Slate*.)

The point: Creative sanctions that fit the problem, address the structural issue, and result from our using criminal and civil cases as a way to leverage reform is what we should aspire to. Imagine if the prosecutorial response to the subprime crisis had been to force real reform on that sector in terms of how subprime loans were marketed and sold. Imagine if major banks had been forced by prosecutors to change the way they handled all securitization. Imagine if prosecutors had really forced the rating agencies to grade honestly—by putting structural relief in place, instead of just asking for some money back. Those would have been meaningful remedies.

For me, of course, the initial introduction to all of this had been back in my days of the Manhattan DA's office. It was the Gambino trucking case—and the effort back in 1992 to break the monopoly exercised by organized crime—that got the gears turning about the importance of non-traditional sanctions. (Recall that Sel Raab in his *New York Times* article determined that our effort to break the hold of organized crime had succeeded.) A more traditional response back then would have been limited to jail time and a fine. But that would not have broken organized crime's control over an entire industry.

So Conclusion Three of this chapter is that the range of injunctive relief we impose when corporations have been involved in structural wrongdoing must be vastly expanded. Jail and money only go so far: Creative injunctive relief can change things more dramatically!

Let me also suggest a few other significant changes in our use of remedies that we should think about: As I said at the top of this chapter, corporations like the upside of personhood but do not want the risks and responsibilities that flow from it. So let's try giving corporations the same exposure that seems to be working so well for individuals: three strikes and you're out, or even capital punishment. (Although, to be clear, I oppose the death penalty in cases other than terrorism and treason, because of the risk of error in our judicial system.) Recidivism is a major problem for our financial sector: Let's stamp it out.

In 1986, as a junior Assistant District Attorney, I was assigned to the Career Criminal Unit—where we brought special attention to bear on recidivist felons. Those who satisfied the parameters of being repeat offenders, we felt, deserved special prosecutorial focus. And, when they were convicted, we sought special sanctions that were harsher and hence more likely to protect society from their pernicious behavior.

The system worked. (I am not endorsing the aberrant use of three strikes for minor offenders, which has often produced wild injustice.) And while it was merely one among the many theories of prosecution and policing that were brought to bear on our crime problem, the focus on recidivist felons was one that had unique effectiveness. Violent felonies committed by repeat offenders led to prison sentences that kept the offenders off the street for a long time—often until the realistic end of their potential criminal lives.

It is time to bring this same principle to bear on our corporate offenders.

Imagine that a major bank were found responsible—civilly or criminally—sequentially, for lying about stock recommendations, participating in LIBOR rate fixing, and knowingly marketing bad mortgage debt: Shouldn't that bank face the same sort of "three strikes and you're out" logic that even petty criminals sometimes face? Only good would result. Temporary disruption would quickly settle back as others filled the void left by corporations who felt they were indispensable or deemed "too big to prosecute" by Eric Holder. As DeGaulle said, the graveyards are filled with indispensable men. So too would we recover from the disappearance of "indispensable" corporations. Others will underwrite, analyze, or advise. But the Sword of Damocles would hang over those who until now had felt impervious. Recidivism would be reduced dramatically if we applied this rule to corporate defalcations.

The lesson from the career criminal unit applies to corporations as well as street thugs. Longer sentences, real sanctions, and even the threat of capital punishment work. Corporations want to be people. Let's acknowledge they have First Amendment rights, but let's also use the tools of sanctions we use against mere individuals against them as well. We should treat recidivist corporations like recidivist individuals—a life sentence that is akin to capital punishment. They will take note.

So let's sum up:

- **First**: Criminal sanctions and the corporate death penalty should be used against corporations more often.
- **Second**: As part of any agreement when structured fraud has been committed, senior management and executives should be required to depart—if they have overseen systemic violations which they failed to see or alter. One of the most galling aspects to the aftermath of the 2008 cataclysm was that senior management at each of the major bailed-out institutions remained. It was as if they had done no wrong. Because their decisions were not deemed criminally

wrong, they were left in place. That was obviously an improper standard. Bailouts without management shifts were an error in judgment—as would be any resolution of structural wrong doing at any
major bank without requiring managerial changes.

- **Third**: Structural reform imposed through injunctive relief should
  be part of any judicial resolution: Without addressing the structural reasons the crimes were committed, we ensure they will occur
  again. What made the Gambino, Marsh, Glaxo, and mutual fund
  settlements useful was the effort at structural reform. Given the recidivism rate we are seeing in the financial services sector, it is fair
  to conclude that the settlements imposed over the past several years
  have not provided a sufficient deterrent to continued violations of
  law. We must clearly embrace the notion that we should change the
  way things are done through imposing injunctive relief.
- **Fourth**: No more "neither admit nor deny." Settlements that permit
  companies to "neither admit nor deny" wrongdoing are transpar-
  ently based on a simple risk analysis by the company and should not
  be afforded the imprimatur of a judicial seal of approval. As a lawyer
  for SAC Capital said when explaining a $602 million proposed settle-
  ment: "We're willing to pay $600 million because we have a business
  to run and don't want this hanging over our heads with litigation
  that could last for years." Litigation between private citizens may
  be about money, and hence require no admission of wrongdoing at
  its conclusion. Yet if the government brings a civil case and exacts a
  payment, that payment must be accompanied by a rationale other
  than a mere cost-benefit analysis. The predicate to governmental
  intervention in the first place is that a wrong was committed, and
  extracting a payment without some acknowledgment of that reality
  turns the government's action into little more than a tax.

Judge Victor Marrero of the Southern District of New York recently
wrote about this, in the context of the proposed settlement between
SAC Capital and the SEC:

> "A few other qualities about these events bear comment. In the
> real world, and in the eyes of the public whose perceptions pass
> judgment on official actions, harmful conduct on the scale of the
> contemporary models ordinarily does not occur absent some
> form of wrongdoing; the damage the victims suffer cannot always
> be blamed on acts of God or the mischief of leprechauns. For the
> people directly injured, and for others who share an interest in
> these matters implicating broad public concerns, the purposes of
> the justice system embodied in compensation, deterrence, and
> punishment cannot be adequately satisfied, and there cannot be

proper closure when incidents causing extensive loss occur, if the individuals or entities responsible for the large-scale wrongful consequences are not properly held accountable. These impressions hold doubly true in situations, such as may apply in the case at hand, where strong evidence of wrongdoing exists, or where at least circumstantially, as embodied in the doctrine of res ipsa loquitur, the events are unlikely to have happened without substantial misconduct. ... In this Court's view, it is both counterintuitive and incongruous for defendants in this SEC enforcement action to agree to settle a case for over $600 million that would cost a fraction of that amount, say $1 million, to litigate, while simultaneously declining to admit the allegations asserted against it by the SEC. An outside observer viewing these facts could readily conclude that CR Intrinsic and the Relief Defendants essentially folded, in exchange for the SEC's concession enabling them to admit no wrongdoing."

Judicial hesitancy to approve settlements that "neither admit nor deny" will—and should—only grow as a judicial imprimatur is used to mask crass business decisions to which the SEC is now a party. I hope that the new leadership at the SEC will mandate that an admission of guilt is a necessary part of future settlements in cases of this stature or magnitude. The law and justice require such an acknowledgment—or else nothing has been accomplished.

Corporations want the rights of personhood; let's also give them the sanctions that accompany personhood.

8

WASTING THE CRISIS

Rule Eight:
You can do a lot of things
right,
and still lose.

A crisis may be a terrible thing to waste—as we have been told so often. But we essentially have. Now that a few years have passed since the cataclysm of 2008, it is useful to make a first evaluation of how we fared in accomplishing the three essential post-crisis objectives: 1) resuscitate the economy at a moment when it was in apparent free fall; 2) reform the industry that was primarily responsible for creating the crisis, in an effort to prevent the sorts of risks and misallocation of capital that metastasized into the crisis from occurring again; and 3) impose sanctions on those whose behavior—either collectively, individually, or organizationally—merited sanctions. The bottom line? We get a passing but not exemplary grade on the first objective, and a failing grade on each of the next two.

I do not want here to try to recount here the years of regulatory and capital market leadership failures that led us to the precipice in 2008. Though not designed to focus exclusively on that specific issue, the prior chapters may have shed some light on those failures. Each of the myths about economic theory that I have tried to debunk was accepted in full by those directing our financial system as we approached 2008. From Alan Greenspan to Tim Geithner, a false intellectual model drove their decisions—and they battled mightily to defend that model even as the facts made the case impossible. From the core notions of deregulation and self-regulation to the ability of new private sector risk models to handle crazy leverage ratios, the intellectual principles that underlay the pre-2008 world were fatally flawed.

For a more comprehensive telling of that story, I believe the best recitations of the macroeconomic story are provided by any of the following volumes: Paul Krugman, *The Return of Depression Economics and the Crisis of 2008*; Joseph Stiglitz, *Freefall: America, Free Markets, and the Sinking of the World Economy*; John Cassidy, *How Markets Fail: The Logic of Economic Calamities*; Joe Nocera and Bethany Mclean, *All the Devils Are Here: The Hidden History of the Financial Crisis*; Gretchen Morgenson and Joshua Rosner, *Reckless Endangerment: How Outsized Ambition, Greed, and Corruption Led to Economic Armageddon*; Charles Ferguson, *Predator Nation: Corporate Criminals, Political Corruption, and the Hijacking of America*; and Sheila Bair, *Bull by the Horns: Fighting to Save Main Street from Wall Street, and Wall Street from Itself.* For those of us who prefer watching to reading, there is of course the stupendous Academy Award-winning "Inside Job," by Charles Ferguson. These accounts are rich in detail and will give one a cardio workout by inciting anger and concern at the lapses in both our public regulatory structure and our private sector leadership.

Yet what did we do once at the precipice? Let's take a quick tour through the three objectives.

FIRST: RESUSCITATING THE ECONOMY

How did we respond when we needed to resuscitate the economy? Essentially we did so in a one-dimensional and inadequate way. There were two aspects to this response: First, the guarantees and bailouts, and second, the stimulus.

FUNDING THE BANKS

With virtually unlimited guarantees and cash infusions, we threw as much cash as possible at the financial services sector. Every aspect of the banking sector was guaranteed by the government, to ensure that the freeze that had set in did not lead to a complete shutdown of the gears of commerce. From money market funds, to all bank deposits, to commercial paper, all were guaranteed; each of the major banks was given an unconditional federal guarantee; the multitude of guarantees were designed to backstop all the risk in the system. The magnitude of these outlays—which go way beyond TARP itself—were approximated by *The New York Times* as follows, as of April 30, 2011: $12.2 trillion committed, $2.5 trillion spent, and $10 billion collected in dividends and fees.

At the moment of extremis, most of the major money-center financial institutions would have collapsed absent government intervention. Although Goldman still maintains that it could have survived the freeze in the credit markets, I doubt it. All these entities depend upon short-term borrowing—from overnight to 30-day—and those markets totally froze. There was an emotional equivalent to a "bank run" on short-term lending to banks, and the dominos would have fallen sequentially and rapidly without the government guarantees. Consequently, the banks were given a lifeline. Providing this guarantee was necessary and appropriate at the moment of extremis. Those who simply wanted to stand by and do nothing at that moment are speaking from either an unbridled populism that while emotionally satisfying would have been disastrous, or a failure to recognize the consequences of the sequence of events that would have followed.

But the way these guarantees were implemented reflected the essential intellectual error that was made by those at the top: they confused the financial sector with the entire economy. They presumed that if the banks and the non-bank banks were nursed back to health the rest of the economy would follow quickly. Not so. They acted as though merely pushing enough cash into the financial sector to ensure that they would be liquid would resuscitate lending and demand. The much deeper damage done by the excess leverage that had been baked into the economy was years in undoing—and simply deleveraging the banks by shifting their burden to taxpayers—through bailouts and low interest rates—did not do anything to restore adequate demand to the economy. On top of the fear created by rising unemployment, the destruction of household wealth from the combined collapse of the housing and equity markets—the two primary asset classes for middle class America—destroyed consumer demand at a much deeper level. The answer to this problem was available to the government at that moment: Pair the bank bailouts with an obligation for mortgage relief and structural reform in the finance sector. But more on that below.

Just as critical, many of the calls that were made, while of necessity made with alacrity, have never been explained and were fundamentally amiss. For instance, the decision to give Goldman a check for $12.8 billion—to cover its entire exposure to AIG—is simply mystifying. Was the decision designed to give Goldman the cash it needed to survive, despite its claim that it didn't need any cash, or to cover its full exposure to AIG's risk of default? And if the latter, why? (For much more on the inconsistent answers to these questions at the Fed, Treasury, and Goldman, see several of my *Slate* articles.) This $12.8 billion, parenthetically, all to one investment bank, is three times as much as we spent to reform our educational system through the much vaunted, and properly praised, "race to the top."

Yet even putting aside the size of these often unexplained cash bailouts and guarantees, many of which were not and will not be repaid, the premise of the mammoth cash outlays was wrong: the belief that simply pushing cash into the financial system would solve that sector's problems—even without fundamental structural reform.

THE STIMULUS

The second aspect of the response to the need to prevent a fall into the abyss—the stimulus—was way too small, and also did not address one of the largest structural drains on demand: the huge mortgage overhang that destroyed the housing market. We are only now seeing a possible, nascent recovery in the housing market. With the economy in free-fall, and consumers overleveraged and fearful that their two primary assets, their houses and their stock portfolios, were severally diminished, it should have been clear that much more significant and more immediate demand stimulus was needed. Consequently, relieving the mortgage overhang was needed both to restore consumer spending and to revive the housing market. The senior economic advisers to the President realized this but somehow failed to act on their understanding of the true magnitude of the crisis we were facing. But again, this was because too much focus was on the financial institutions, not consumers or "regular" people. The economy, as a result, was put on only an anemic road to recovery.

Having said that, the argument of the "right" that the stimulus didn't work is totally false. Keynes was vindicated; the additional fiscal contribution mattered:

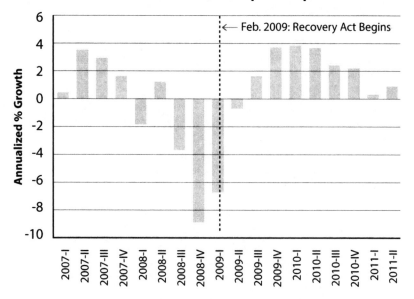

Real GDP Growth, 2007q1-2011q2

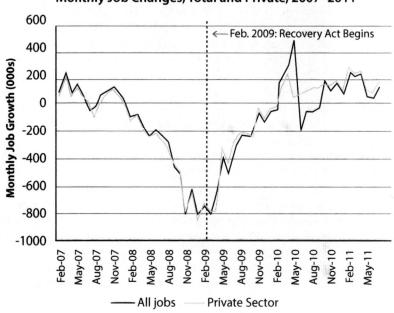

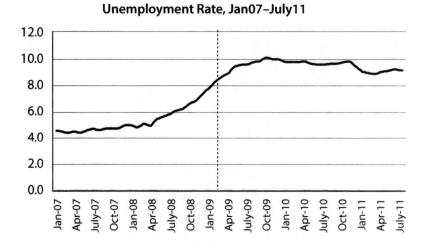

Though inadequate in scope, the stimulus worked. Contrary to so much of the political rhetoric that accompanied the public outrage as manifested in the elections of 2010—essentially outrage at the banks being bailed out while so many others remained underwater or unemployed—the macro effect of the stimulus was to stop the economic collapse and put us on a frustratingly slow path to normalcy. Had the stimulus been appropriately sized, the recovery would have been faster, sharper and more complete. See "Could We Have Had a Bigger Stimulus," by Ezra Klein, in *The Washington Post.*

As the history is being written, with some accuracy, the response of bailouts and a sizable (yet still not sufficient) stimulus saved us from a deeper abyss than we might otherwise have fallen into; yet the same flawed vision of those who had created the structures that led to the crisis of 2008 also led them to simply extend additional capital to those same institutions, supporting with tax dollars the public assumption of risk that permitted the institutions to escape great pain. Indeed, one of the reports of the Special Inspector General for TARP concluded that the TARP funds were merely leading to a continuation of the outsized risk taking that had preceded the crash: "A significant legacy of TARP is increased moral hazard and potentially disastrous consequences associated with institutions deemed 'too big to fail.' ... A recent working paper from Federal Reserve economists confirms that TARP encouraged high-risk behavior by insulating the risk takers from the consequences of failure—which is known as moral hazard."

The White House and Treasury Department, had they focused on the mortgage crisis, would also have realized that the banks' need for capital created the perfect but transitory opportunity to resolve the mortgage crisis. At that very moment—when the banks needed additional capital from the public—we should have negotiated hard and gotten something significant back in return. And that "something" should have been double barreled: banking reform and mortgage relief for homeowners.

The banks should have been offered the following deal, on a one-time take-it-or-leave-it basis: Here is the capital you need to return to solvency; here are the deposit guarantees that will ensure depositor confidence and lower your borrowing costs; here is the dramatic reduction in all interest costs that also amount to a huge transfer of wealth from savers to the banks, so that you will be able to pay your salaries and perhaps even dividends over the next five years. But in return you must agree first to structural reform of the sector, and second to the refinancing of mortgages so that the housing market is restored to some stability, and consumer demand can begin to perk up. The banks—of necessity—would have agreed. It would have been the "grand bargain" and "rough justice" that would have saved our economy. And it would have been far better policy as well. (For additional, reading, try *The Bankers' New Clothes:*

What's Wrong With Banking and What to Do About It, by Anat Admati and Martin Hellwig.)

Just so it is clear: The critical piece of mortgage reform would have been principal reduction. Changing foreclosure practices—such as those revealed in the so-called "robo-signing" scandal—are hugely important, but pale in comparison to the macro impact of principal reduction. That the idea was mentioned so rarely early on shows the intellectual grip that was held by status quo bankers on our leadership. Writing down any obligations other than their own was somehow viewed as antithetical to the principles of capitalism.

Oddly, the most frequent response to a call for mortgage reductions has been invocation of the "moral hazard" argument. It was claimed that we should not reward the bad behavior of those who had borrowed too much. There is, of course, an element of truth to that concern. But the refinancing could have been arranged such that any subsequent sale of the house which resulted in a profit could have been divided with the lending entity, giving the bank in essence some residual equity in the house in return for the write down of the mortgage. This would have been akin to the conversion of debt to equity—a traditional swap that occurs in corporate refinancing. This would have been fair, and good economics.

To summarize: The stimulus was too small, and the cash and guarantees that were directed at the financial sector were absorbed without any meaningful short-term giveback by the institutions that could have reshaped the housing market. It should be no surprise therefore that a structural demand crisis still limits the economy, and job growth has been slower than in any previous recovery. The damage was deeper in the great recession, yet the magnitude of the therapy did not reflect the scope of the damage to the economy.

Having said all that, we still recovered better than did those nations in Europe that pursued an austerity plan—believing that when government revenues fell they should stop spending. Hoover's intellectual revival has driven the continent into a state of serious continued recession, with unemployment rates currently above 12 percent across the entire Euro zone, and above 27 percent and 26 percent in Greece and Spain respectively. Moreover, growth in Europe has stalled, with Europe now mired in the longest recession since World War II. (See "Euro Crisis Mires Continent in Longest Slump Since War," by Marcus Walker and Brian Blackstone, in *The Wall Street Journal*.) In the past five years we have witnessed one of history's great macroeconomic experiments. As the Europeans tried austerity, we tested Keynes; although our response was too timid, at least we witnessed a revival, while Europe nearly flatlined. The Europeans fell into the trap of listening to deficit hawks, driving their economy further into the abyss.

Let me add one footnote: This critique is not meant to suggest that a multitude of other structural factors have not contributed to the stagnation of job and wage growth over the past years.

SECOND: RESTRUCTURING FINANCE

The second question continues to be a troubling one: Have we restructured the financial services sector sufficiently. The answer is clearly no—and it is not even a close call. What were the primary and obvious structural problems that led to the crisis? Too big to fail, too big to prosecute, too big to manage, excess leverage, OPM, and conflicts of interest that were baked into the business model of too many financial institutions. We have perhaps remedied only one of the structural issues: The grotesque level of leverage that was tolerated by the regulators has been reduced. And that deleveraging, which has been shouldered by savers and taxpayers, will, if history is any lesson, be transitory. But the other problems has very much survived—and arguably have gotten only worse.

- **Very simply, we still have TBTF—and it is worse.** As Richard Fisher, the president of the Dallas Federal Reserve Bank—one of the few Fed voices to push back against increasing concentration—observed in a *Wall Street Journal* op-ed: "A dozen megabanks today control almost 70 percent of the assets in the U.S. banking industry.... Meanwhile a mere 0.2 percent of banks deemed 'too big to fail' are treated differently from the other 99.8 percent, and differently from other businesses. Implicit government policy has made these institutions exempt from the normal process of bankruptcy and creative destruction. Without fear of failure, these banks and their counterparties can take excessive risk.... Thanks to this significant subsidy, the biggest banking organizations, along with their many non-bank subsidiaries (e.g., investment banks, securities lenders, finance companies) grow larger and riskier."

  If we had "socialized the risk and privatized the gain" implicitly before the crash, we have done so explicitly now. Nobody can challenge the data that prove the increasing trend toward accentuated TBTF. The megabankers are struggling to explain—unpersuasively—why somehow next time TBTF will not have the dangerous radiating impact that it did in 2008. (Take a look at Paul Volcker's speech "Three Years Later: Unfinished Business in Financial Reform.")

  Interestingly, as lacking in creativity as policy makers were in the first few years after the crash, a few are now awakening to the realization that we have rebuilt the same system—and perhaps made it worse by injecting it with steroids. Senators Sherrod Brown and David Vitter have proposed a bill that would address TBTF more aggressively, primarily through much more rigorous capital requirements. (See "In Brown Vitter Bill, a Banking Overhaul With Possible Teeth," by Jesse Eisinger, in *The New York Times*.) Although it is hard to believe that the bill will make any real headway, it is now considered "polite" in the halls of Congress to raise the issue of fundamental reform of TBTF. That was not the case when Geithner initially dictated the terms of the conversation.

- **We now have an explicit "too big to prosecute" policy**—courtesy of Eric Holder and Lanny Breuer. They have created a zone of immunity for TBTF entities, which when combined with the SEC's "neither admit nor deny" strategy creates a bizarre world of see no evil, admit no evil, just pay bonuses.

- **We still have entities too big to manage**—and it is no better at all. If the luster of Jamie Dimon was briefly held out as the counterargument that the right management could navigate through the swamp of TBTF, that luster has not only dimmed, it should by now be fundamentally tarnished. A closer look at JPMorgan Chase—see Rosner, *JP Morgan Chase: Out of Control*—has shown that like every other bank, beneath the sheen of Dimon's PR is a litany of serious management oversights and risk control failures that prove the same fundamental point: Entities of that scale with perverse incentives for risk taking, burden shifting, and access to OPM will continue to be troubled. I will concede that Dimon is a superb manager. That merely reinforces the point. Even he cannot manage the enormity of the tensions that are created in institutions of this size. *Nobody* can manage them properly. Indeed, for a devastating critique of the London Whale debacle as a management case study, read "Lesson Learned After Financial Crisis: Nothing Much Has Changed," by Jesse Eisinger, in *The New York Times*. All of which is part of the reason even Sandy Weill—the father of bank concentration—has now recognized that big banks should be dismantled.

- **Conflicts of interest are still at the root of the so-called "synergies" that underlie the business model of the major banks**. Grubman's brilliant rationalization that "conflicts had become synergies" is still not true—and never will be. The cross-selling—whether it is in-house mutual fund products to depositors or stocks to unknowing investors—is still problematic and ripe for abuse. Given the reality that such a large percentage of bank revenue is fee-driven these days, it is hard for a customer to be confident that any advice is little more than a fee generator, rather than a legitimate offer of wisdom. Add on top of this the reality, as made evident by Goldman witnesses in front of Senator Carl Levin, that even the

so-called "best and brightest" couldn't explain who their client was
or what duty they owed the client, it is clear that banking is still an
ethical swamp.

- **We still have OPM on steroids.** Because of the continuing federal guarantees we have been discussing, the major banks have
lower borrowing costs than other institutions. This is the same as
a massive cash subsidy—calculated by Bloomberg News as being
worth $83 BILLION a year. That is a pipeline of money they get to
play with that is not actually theirs—it is a gift we have made to
them. Classic OPM. Also, because the Volcker rule has not yet been
implemented—and when it is, it is likely to have been so watered
down—banks are still using federally guaranteed deposits to fund
their risky investment strategies. Indeed, knowledgeable people
with whom I speak tell me that even now the major banks cannot
properly understand their exposure to the swamp of derivatives
trades they have made on all their existing trading platforms. Their
"net exposure," as they say, is still something of a mystery to them—
and certainly to their regulators. And all of this is made possible and
profitable by their access to capital guaranteed by taxpayers: Their
borrowing is subsidized and the deposits they use for high-risk investments are guaranteed. Bloomberg News editorialized: "The
subsidy is too large, it is bad for the economy, and the best way to
deal with it is through measures such as increased capital requirements. ... The subsidy's exact size is less important than its effects.
By providing an extra measure of insurance to banks that have the
potential to tank the economy, the government encourages them
to become as threatening as possible. In other words, the desire to
mitigate crises undermines the market discipline that would otherwise keep banks from getting so big."

Dodd-Frank was a success only if measured against the initial and
grossly inadequate plan proffered from the White House throughout
the process. Geithner, it is now well understood, never wanted real
structural reform—or any meaningful limits on bank size, or even a
Volcker rule. Only because Barney Frank and outside advocacy groups
pushed for some elements of risk control was any regulatory power really increased.

But at the end of the day, the bill stands as exhibit one for what I call
the "legislative charade." Every crisis requires a resolution that provides
the powers that should have prevented the crisis both deniability for responsibility and the appearance that they have now responded properly.
Hence, we pass bills designed to give each of the relevant parties a story
of exculpation: Regulators can claim—falsely—that with new powers
just granted them they will have the power they lacked before to stop the

dangerous behavior. Regulators of course had the power before; most just didn't want to use it. By passing the bill Congress gets to show action, even though its primary role as the crisis brewed was to inhibit regulatory action, by lobbying on behalf of the financial entities. Just look at the many times Congress, both through statutory action and lobbying, asked or demanded that regulators—from federal to state attorneys general—not intervene! And the President gets to sign a bill portending a new era of aggressive intervention, even though it was his own regulators who had failed to use the sufficient power they had to forestall the bad stuff that metastasized into the crisis—think of the OCC and the SEC. And of course, the private sector now gets to blame the regulators as well, claiming that the regulators should have seen the crisis coming and if they had been sufficiently empowered the regulators would have stopped the bad acts. So while Dodd-Frank has some very useful provisions—the Volcker Rule and Living Will provisions relating to systemically important financial institutions being the most central—we should never forget the imperatives that were satisfied by its passage.

Our effort at reform has failed, which means that as soon as leverage ratios begin to creep up again, all the elements of another crisis will be in place.

THIRD: SANCTIONS, ANYONE?

Third, and finally—did we sanction anybody, individually, collectively, or organizationally? The answer to this is pretty clear. Now, as discussed in Chapter Seven, sanctioning corporations is not easy, and throughout my career I have struggled with both the desire to impose sanctions that would provide individual and general deterrence and also provide the requisite degree of structural reform and "justice." Yet as the many cases I discuss above have shown, this is not always easy. Did the deal with the Gambinos serve justice? Did the overarching deal with the investment banks with regard to analytical research—the global settlement—serve justice? Did our effort to send more people to jail in the mutual fund and insurance bid rigging case do more? I do not pretend that I can give a simple, or unbiased, answer to any of these questions.

But I will say this. After the crash of 2008, the DOJ and the U.S. Attorney's Offices around the nation failed. They did not bring either the structural cases designed to prevent the types of conflicts and fraud that had led to the cataclysm in the first instance, OR the individual cases against the decision-makers who set up the misleading deals or fraudulent appraisals, or who made the misleading statements about the many products being improperly sold. There is ample evidence that the U.S. Attorney's Offices simply lacked the desire to make these cases or even the belief that they should be made.

Securitizations that were knowingly oversold were ripe for criminal fraud cases. Yet our prosecutorial authorities failed to bring to bear the fervor, creativity, or sense of understanding of what occurred on Wall Street in the investigations or charging decisions. Instead, they simply bought into the defense of the street that people misunderstood the market and made mistakes. That is false. As the Abacus deal with Goldman and the many cases that had a similar structure made clear, to a great extent the daisy chain of bad loans, securitization, bond ratings, and playing with OPM was a knowing and easy way to shed risk and play games that constituted a massive fraud on the market. Yet not until years later, after much public pressure, after the Clayton documents were aired by the Financial Crisis Inquiry Commission and many commentators spent time challenging the federal government to respond, were a few and inadequate cases brought. And even then, the cases were against the rating agencies, not the banks themselves.

As I have made clear, even if seeking traditional criminal or even civil sanctions against the senior management of the banks was not easy, at a minimum when extending the bailout funds, a condition should have been a change of management. Instead, the awful image of the same leadership that had blithely led us over the precipice accepting bailouts, pocketing their bonuses shortly thereafter, and continuing on their way, while refusing to write down the mortgages of innocent borrowers, merely accentuated to the public that justice had failed. Sheila Bair tells the devastating story of how the first question of John Thain—then Merrill Lynch's CEO—when being told that his bank would receive a $10 billion capital infusion from the federal government was: Will this affect my compensation? Even if all they were responsible for were massive errors in judgment, that should have been enough to have these executives removed. Interestingly, when General Motors was bailed out, its CEO was removed. The dichotomy has never been well explained.

In sum, I have rarely been as disappointed in our Justice Department as I have been over the past five years. They define lethargy and inadequacy—not creativity and understanding. As a consequence, since the crisis of 2008 it is not surprising that there have been a continuing stream of additional corporate violations: from the LIBOR scandal, to money laundering, to massive Foreign Corrupt Practices Act violations that await prosecution, significant and high-level frauds have continued to emerge. This suggests that the claim by those in the executive suite that "we have learned the lesson" is unfortunately not accurate. It is hard to conclude that we did anything other than fail in our third postcrisis objective—the search for accountability.

The bottom line: We have unfortunately wasted this crisis. Does that mean another inevitably awaits? If one reads and believes Galbraith, the answer is probably yes. It may be a few years off, but put on your seat belt!

9

FINAL THOUGHTS

The foundation

of the

conservative economic ideology

has failed

Part of what has emerged from this volume, I hope, is an argument that the "market" as it was explained and described to the general public during the era that began with President Reagan and ended in the crash of 2008 was a mere caricature of what markets really are, and how they have to be understood. The foundation pieces of the dogma that were promoted to justify the destruction of government's affirmative role in the marketplace were too facile—and often simply wrong. Yet in an era when the wages for most Americans were stagnating, making the burden of taxes the target of public resentment was a powerful and effective political strategy. Taxes and the government became the enemy. What resulted was an era where government enforcement of the rules of the market was eviscerated, and although government spending as a percentage of GDP remained relatively stable, government revenues as a percentage of GDP dropped to near post-WW2 lows. This drove deficits skyward. These structural deficits were then exacerbated by the costs of two wars—Iraq and Afghanistan—and stimulus spending after the cataclysm of 2008, pushing deficits to levels beyond what we were accustomed to accept. The ensuing political battles were acrimonious and by and large prevented rational discourse about genuine cause and effect.

Yet several points should be clear to those who want to be thoughtful and analytical about policy as we go forward. Putting ideology aside, we should all be able to agree on certain core principles from the historical record of the past decades:

- **The near unitary focus on lowering tax rates over the past 30 years is predicated on a false premise:** That our marginal rates are so high that hard work is being discouraged, limiting economic growth. In fact, the evidence is pretty clear that raising and lowering marginal rates over the past several decades has neither driven workers out of the productive economy, nor enticed them in. Indeed the periods of our greatest and most consistent economic growth were at times when marginal rates were much higher than they are now. Yet the revenue we have lost has starved certain public investment we need in critical areas to remain competitive.

- **The concept of "market failure" is as much a part of the intellectual foundation of "free markets" as is the notion that supply and demand curves intersect to give us the right price and level of output of any product.** Externalities—such as from air pollution at a power plant—are one critical example of such a market failure. Overcoming these market failures requires that government set up rules that subsidize some behavior, tax others, and outright forbid some. Much of the government intervention that is protested—by businesses in particular—is meant to recognize and deal with the negative externalities these very businesses have created.

- **Self-regulation never has been much more than an oxymoron—and never will be.** A vigorous role for government enforcement is a pre-condition to maintaining any standards of ethics and integrity in the marketplace. Those who invoke self-regulation most vigorously have unfortunately come from the sectors that have given us the greatest defalcations and frauds in recent history.

- **Competition is a necessary prerequisite for a market and innovation—yet the drive to stymie and undercut competition is part and parcel of many business models—**and has been throughout the history of capitalism. Indeed, maybe it should be the goal of many businesses. The consequence is that aggressive government enforcement of anti-monopolistic behavior is critical for markets to survive.

- **The respect for fiduciary relationships has waned—yet these fiduciary duties are even more important today than they once were**, because our increasingly complex and interconnected economy is now even more based on "agency" relationships than was once the case. The failure of these agency relationships can explain much of what has gone wrong in our corporate or governmental sectors. The notion that "conflicts have become synergies" has become a corrosive excuse to create business models and permit practices that eviscerated the core integrity of many institutions. Wall Street in particular became the home of such rationalization.

- **As the finance sector grew in both scale and profitability, it embraced dangerous structural flaws.** Most critically, leverage levels were way beyond what was rational, and incentives to embrace risk with other people's money—"OPM"—encouraged misallocation of capital and the inflation of asset bubbles. In addition, banks grew much larger as a percentage of GDP than had ever been permitted, creating dangerous conflicts and tensions. Only marginal progress at best has been made in remedying these structural issues.
- **Corporations may be people, but we haven't yet figured out how to sanction them as people.** Until we do, they are getting the rights and privileges of personhood without the obligations. That equation does not work.
- **The conservative argument for the "devolution" of power from the federal government to states, the so-called "new federalism," was really a facade used to argue against any governmental intervention in the marketplace.** The moment states began to use the power that conservatives supposedly believed they should possess, arguments for "pre-emption" emerged, and the core concept of federalism was turned on its head.

A PROGRESSIVE AGENDA

IS HARDER IN THE 21ST CENTURY

THAN IN THE 20TH

Even as we see the distribution of income getting more and more unequal, and can agree that our social contract calls for some form of remedial action, solutions are harder than they once were. The simple answers of a more educated workforce and investment in the infrastructure that undergirds private entrepreneurship do not produce the dramatic increases in wealth spread across the entire economy that they once did. Labor now competes globally, replaced by new technological means of production, making it harder and harder for those who do not control capital or have a unique skill in the labor market to raise their standard of living. Even as some of our cost disadvantages—such as in pure labor costs, or the cost of energy—dissipate with respect to China, for instance, the jobs created in "new" manufacturing are not sufficiently numerous to overcome the massive out-migration of jobs over the past several decades. The anxiety that results has produced a politics that is edgier and less compatible with compromise. Negative-sum politics is harder than positive-sum politics. Simply making the tax code more progressive, investing in our intellectual capital, and assisting workers in organizing, though worthy ideas and objectives, will not move us nearly as far as they once did, given the realities of the new world economic order. Hence the seemingly intractable movement of income toward those at the top. The 1 percent keep doing better.

Our advantages will continue to be in the domains of innovative ideas and technologies—where we can create new markets and modes of production. Although these will not have the same ripple effects through the economy as auto production once did, for instance, it is nonetheless where we must invest. Consequently, although the comparative advantage we have in many areas is now less than it once was, this is still the primary means of moving forward. Should we purse the other policy objectives as well—raising the minimum wage, a more progressive tax code, of course. But investment in intellectual capital and the infrastructure of ideas—R & D, universities—are far and away the most critical investments we can make.

RULES FOR LIFE

We have an infatuation with lists in our media and culture, and David Letterman has turned the idea of a Top 10 list into an iconic part of our late-night, often gallows humor. So in an effort to provide something that is less technocratic than some of the prior chapters—which have been perhaps too heavy in economic jargon—here are some thoughts that are takeaways from the past several years. Perhaps even a set of rules to aspire to live by:

1. **Loyalty and fiduciary duty matter.** Our failures—political and personal—over the past years have followed from a simple inability to be loyal to duties we know we have, yet still fail to respect.

2. **Incentives matter.** We can almost always predict how someone will act when we see how their financial incentives have been arranged. So let's create incentives that comport with the outcomes we want, and get rid of those that create an impulse to act contrary to the rules of integrity and sound judgment that we value.

3. **Techies, not politicians, have changed the world.** Although we cover the political world with excessive attention to often meaningless detail, I am hard pressed to think of a truly original idea that has emanated from the political arena over the past two decades. On the other hand, the technological revolution has been real, transformative, and more remarkable than science fiction. The Internet might just be the modern analog of the Gutenberg press—sparking access to information, thought, and wisdom in a way that generates a modern renaissance. So let's acknowledge that we spend too

much time focused on the meaningless words of politicians, and not enough on the truly creative parts of our society.

4. **Hubris is terminal.** Or as DeGaulle stated it, the graveyards are filled with indispensable men. Our sense of self-importance is not only grossly overrated, but can generate a dangerous arrogance in decision making that often ends poorly. It is amazing that institutions manage to continue onward even after the most essential people move on.

5. **Spotting inflection points is true wisdom.** History, markets, and politics almost never move in straight lines. The truly smart folks understand the dynamics that lie beneath apparently straight lines, and manage to be ahead of the proverbial curve. Whatever domain one operates in, seeing the bend in the curve defines true intellect.

6. **It is better to go down fighting than not to fight at all**, though there can sometimes be only a fine line between courage and stupidity. While I chose to battle aggressively—winning sometimes, not always—I look back still preferring to have fought than not. I would gladly take the scars of battle over the timidity Roosevelt referred to in those "poor and timid souls who knew neither victory nor defeat." The credit does, indeed, go to those "in the arena" who "strive valiantly." Further, I fought up, with those more powerful than I, not down, picking on those weaker. That, I think, is a fundamental divide in life.

7. **Don't bring a pencil to a knife fight.** Said another way: Never play defense. Know the terms of battle, and fight fire with fire. I found out the hard way that using the wrong armament can lead to Pyrrhic victories. Winning in the courts or even on the editorial page many months after the other side has used a vicious and dissembling PR war to destroy does one no good. And a corollary to this might be that "the media descend from the hills to kill the wounded." Perceived weakness begets weakness due to the way the world sees what has transpired. Once one is playing defense, it is very hard to recover.

8. **Change is hard—and rarely comes over tea and crumpets.** No force is as powerful as the status quo. The capacity of entrenched interest groups to retain their benefits—of any sort—is hard to overestimate. The battles are fierce, and leave scars that run deep.

9. **Politics should be a cause, not a profession.** And pragmatism alone is neither a cause nor an ideology. Those in politics merely to survive and retain power may succeed at an elementary level, but will fail in the deeper sense of being transformative or memorable. I respect those who view governance as a cause driven endeavor, even if I disagree with them, as opposed to those for whom mere survival is the objective.

10. **It is better to be Tigger than Eeyore.** If all wisdom is ultimately found in children's books, let this last morsel be that choice bit: Even on the darkest day it is better to have a spring in one's step, and a sense of adventure in one's mind, than to be overcome by the gloom and darkness of cynicism and doubt.

AFTERWORD

GREED IS
NOT
A SOCIAL CONTRACT

For several years I taught a course on political philosophy and politics at The City College of New York, the superb public university that has spawned generations of creativity and leaders in multiple fields. In putting together the syllabus, I thought it made sense to begin with what is perhaps one of the more fundamental questions we have to confront in both politics and economics: How do we distribute income, and why? This chapter is a narrative of the Socratic dialogue I would try to have with my students in thinking about this thorny question at the beginning of the class, updated with more recent data and more recent political analogies. While I could have logically put this as the first chapter in this volume, I thought it fit better as a coda, a last question for us all to grapple with as we think about the larger issues of public policy. So here goes:

From "Greed is good," the infamous incantation of Michael Douglas in the movie "Wall Street," to the vilification of the "1 percent" by Occupy Wall Street, the issue of how income and wealth should be distributed has consistently been at the center of our political discourse. As it should be. This moral and philosophical question deserves to be something we think about—and talk about—with regularity. Many call for redistribution—the rich are too rich. Others call for the economic pie to be increased in size, since a rising tide supposedly lifts all ships. Some call for all of the above.

With many different metaphors, and at many differing levels of sophistication, the debate dominates our politics. How we divide income and what incentives we create, through our tax code and governmental expenditures, matter enormously. In their totality, these decisions define what we call our "social contract": the set of rules we accept to figure out who we reward—and how. The "1 percent," the "47 percent," the "middle class"? Who is it we most protect, encourage, support, or tax?

For academics this is partly the debate between two giants of modern philosophy—John Rawls and Robert Nozick. In the presidential campaign it was also the debate over "who built that." Was it the "we" we heard about at the Democratic convention—a community of effort that created the foundation for all individual success; or the "I" we heard about at the Republican convention—the entrepreneur whose individual drive and efforts create wealth.

The factual backdrop to the debate is that we have gone, unfortunately and metaphorically, from a bell curve to a barbell in the distribution of income and wealth in the United States. While for many years the middle class was growing and the greatest wealth accretion was to those in the middle of our income distribution, since the 2008 cataclysm 93 percent of the wealth created has accrued to the top 1 percent. Measured by any metric, over the past thirty years we have allocated more and more to fewer and fewer.

Middle-class income has been stagnant since the 1970s, and has declined in the past decade (see Chart 1 below). And the percentage of total income going to the "middle class" has declined as well: See Chart 2.

Median household income has declined over past decade, had stagnated for previous 20 years

Income for the typical middle-class household has stagnated over the past few decades and has actually fallen over the past 10 years: Median income for households—meaning half of the population makes more and half makes less—only grew by 1.6 percent during the supposedly good economic recovery of 2001 to 2007, and it fell by 4.2 percent during the Great Recession of 2007–2009. All told, median annual household income dropped $3,700 over the past decade, falling from $53,164 in 2000 to $49,445 in 2010.

Median household income (2010 dollars)

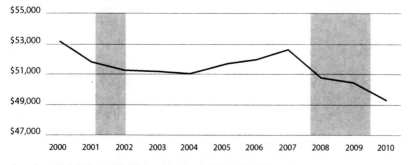

Source: Economic Policy Institute analysis of U.S. Census Bureau Data, shaded bars indicate NBER recession.

Center for American Progress

Share of the nation's income going to the middle class has been declining for decades

As a result of stagnant incomes for the middle class and rising incomes for the rich, the share of the total national income earned by the middle 60 percent of households has been on the decline for decades. It is near its lowest level today since the government began keeping track of the statistic in the late 1960s. In 1968 the middle class received 53.2 percent of the nation's income. By 2010, that share had fallen to 46.5 percent.

Share of Income going to the middle 60 percent of households

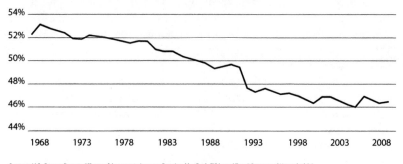

Sources: U.S. Census Bureau, "Share of Aggregate Income Received by Each Fifth and Top 5 Percent of Households"

Center for American Progress

The consequence has been a distribution of wealth that is staggeringly inequitable:

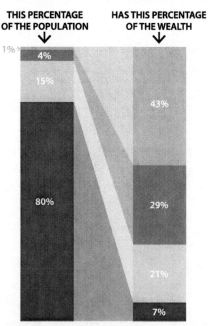

THE DISTRIBUTION OF WEALTH IN THE UNITED STATES

Chart: Michael DeGusta, TheUnderstatement.com - March 2011
Data: From 2007, as per http://sociology.ucsc.edu/whorulesamerica/power/wealth.html

Perhaps the single most important chart that explains the causation underlying this growing reallocation of wealth and the proceeds of growth
is this one:

It explains the following chart: Corporate profits as a percentage of GDP
are at an all-time high. (This also explains the performance of the stock
market recently.)

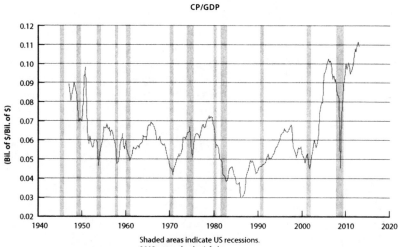

And wages as a percentage of GDP are at an all-time LOW.

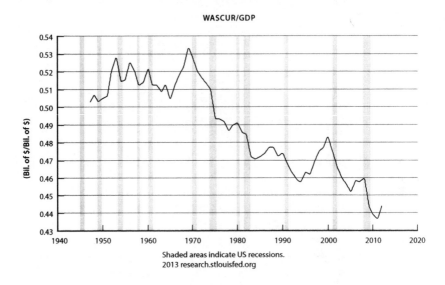

WASCUR/GDP

Shaded areas indicate US recessions.
2013 research.stlouisfed.org

Introductory economics courses teach that increases in worker productivity generate increased output and wealth that are reflected in proportional increases in wages. A 5 percent increase in productivity will generate a 5 percent increase in wages. This is taught as a core principle of economics—and until now it was not only true, but it made common sense: As workers increase their output by a given percentage, they get paid a roughly equivalent percentage increase. And the Productivity vs. Compensation chart above reflects that reality—until about 1975, when wages flat-lined. Even though productivity continued to rise, making U.S. workers the most productive in the world, real wages have barely budged.

Why? Several factors converged, most importantly globalization and technology. The "flat earth" and the opening of vast new regions for production—brilliantly defined by Tom Friedman—changed the competitive landscape for U.S. labor. The negotiation between capital and labor was, and has continued to be, fundamentally altered by the combination of new technologies that are often reducing the demand for labor, increasing the capacity to outsource, and accelerating the decline in labor union power in many core U.S. sectors. Unions now represent a scant 11.3 percent of all U.S. workers. These trends have been accentuated by a U.S. policy of trade liberalization that again created greater opportunities for capital to move freely around the world, and for foreign production to displace U.S. production. Michael Spence, a Nobel-winning economist, calculated that over the past twenty years in the "tradable" sector we have lost 20 million jobs.

Adding several billion additional workers to the global labor force has commoditized much of the U.S. work force, which now must compete against workers in China, India, or any of the new frontiers that are now part of an integrated world economy. In many of these nations, of course, labor does not have any of the protections relating to health, safety, or limits on hours that were at the core of what the U.S. work force had fought for, and come to expect, over prior decades. The consequence has been reflected in the charts above: Corporate profits have grown, and even rebounded swiftly after the cataclysm of 2008, while U.S. wages have been stagnant.

This stagnation of wages as the return to capital has grown has generated the increased share of income and wealth that has accrued to those at the top of society.

All of this has made the debate about our social contract—who gets what and who deserves what—that much more contentious. It is harder to divide a pie that seems to be stagnant or shrinking than it is to divide one that is growing. Against this new economic backdrop, the debate about taxes and spending has become shrill, to say the least. We are living in a world of negative-sum politics, not the positive-sum politics we had grown accustomed to during periods of prosperity.

The heart of our debate usually focuses on who bears the burden of paying for our government—is there a tension between who pays and who benefits? Is the system of paying therefore redistributive, and if so, fairly or unfairly? Despite a fair bit of rhetoric to the contrary, the data show that the percentage of taxes paid by each income group is roughly proportional to the income derived:

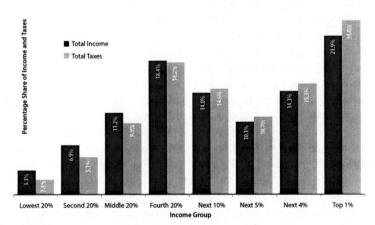

Shares of Total Taxes Paid by Each Income Group Will Be Similar to ther Shares of Income in 2013

Source: Institute on Taxation and Economic Policy (ITEP) Tax Model, April 2013
Citizens for Tax Justice, April 2013

And over time the top marginal tax rate has dropped dramatically.

The meme repeated endlessly by those on the right that the "47 percent" don't pay—recall the infamous tape from the Romney presidential campaign?—is simply false. When one includes payroll taxes, sales taxes, property taxes, and all the other various extractions that government has imposed, the tax burden is roughly proportional to income earned. The top "1 percent" of income earners garner 21 percent of all income and pay 21.6 percent of all taxes; the middle 20 percent earn 11.4 percent of all income and pay 10.3 percent of all taxes, and the bottom 20 percent earn 3.4 percent of all income and pay 2.1 percent of all taxes.

The impact of policies and structures we have put in place in the past years—through the deregulatory spasm and the creation of tax benefits that accrued primarily to those at the top—transformed a system that used to be more progressive and redistributive into one that is roughly proportional in its impact.

The policies of the past two decades shifted us from a system that was avowedly progressive to one that is essentially neutral. I have observed: Never has so much been done for so few who needed so little.

Yet in order to move the debate forward, we should rise above the political bromides of right and left, and even some of the data, and ask the philosophical question: How *should* we distribute income? And in asking this question, we should understand that at least two competing ideologies, each with a firm intellectual foundation, drive our politics. At one level, we might even think of the political debate that we witnessed during the 2012 presidential race as a proxy battle between these two great thinkers: Rawls and Nozick. No matter how deeply we feel our political passions, neither view should be dismissed as lacking intellectual heft or depth.

So, should we be Rawlsians—redistributive—or should we believe in the libertarian world of Nozick? Here is the brief, Wikipedia-like overview of these two competing philosophies.

Rawls concluded that there were two essential principles of justice: first, the "equality principle," which mandates equality among all individuals in areas we would ordinarily consider "political" freedoms—the rights of speech, association, and such. The second principle is more critical to a conversation about "social contracts." It relates to equality of opportunity, and establishes the "difference principle," which argues that those with similar talents should face roughly similar opportunities and that inequalities, to the extent they exist, should be structured to maximize the position of the least well of member of society. This became known as the "maximin" theory: Our obligation was to maximize the position of the least-well-off.

Nozick, often seen as the father of modern libertarianism, focused not on the issue of equality in distribution of income, but rather on the

notion that the freedom of the individual to control his or her own output made it immoral for others to claim any element of that output—in
a tax or otherwise. This was especially so if the purpose of that tax was
to be redistributive. While he acknowledged the need for a minimalist
state that would emerge organically from the interaction of people, he
rejected the notion that redistributing income or wealth was just—as
long as the initial acquisition of income had itself satisfied certain parameters of elemental justice.

To some, the debate is between "justice" and "virtue." Justice—to supporters of Rawls—means greater equality; concern for those who are
less well off. Virtue—to those in the Nozick camp—means rewarding
the work and productivity of those who create. Each has a morally compelling argument.

Let's test these differing world views. Imagine the following three
possible sets of income distribution, where for the sake of simplicity we
will assume there are only three people to be considered, and only one
year to think about:

YEAR ONE

	A	B	C
Person 1	5	6	4
Person 2	6	6	6
Person 3	7	6	8

Each of the possible distributive possibilities has total income of 18,
so the size of the pie is not at issue. What is at issue is how the income
is allocated. Rawls—following the maxim that we should increase the
income of the least-well-off member of society—would opt for B; his argument would *not* be that the individuals should all have equal income,
but rather that the least-well-off member has a higher income in B than
he does in either Option A or C. A devotee of Nozick would say "I do not
care too much about the choices presented as long as the income derived by each of the individuals reflected the benefits that followed from
his own hard work." And parenthetically, note that a utilitarian—look
at John Stuart Mills' writing—might also be equally disposed to each of
these choices, since the total income in each was 18.

The analysis as applied to one year only, where we do not consider the
dynamic effects of income distribution and taxes, presents a relatively
easy philosophical problem. Easy not in the sense that there is an obvious and morally compelling right or wrong answer, but easy in the sense
that the variables are limited.

Yet the real debate is how income distribution affects overall growth and wealth creation *over time*, not merely in the static analysis of one time period. So now imagine the following scenario: What if—and again this is an IF and a big presumption—you were told that because of the income distribution in Year One and the incentives that were required to get us there (marginal tax rates and government programs) Year Two income for each of the options were as follows:

YEAR TWO			
	A	B	C
Person 1	7	7	7
Person 2	8	7	8
Person 3	9	7	10

Note that total Year Two income is now 24 in A, 21 in B, and 25 in C.

As a first matter, under this hypothesis, accepting all the presumptions just for the sake of the argument, the consequence of Option B's pure equality was to generate only a slight increase in economic output. Total income increased only to 21. If this were to happen, some would surely argue that in our effort to achieve pure equality we had taxed away the gains from hard work and additional productivity, and as a consequence had substantially reduced the incentive to work hard. Total output consequently did not increase by much.

Option A, which had some degree of inequality in Year One, and some incentives attached to retaining income, produced total income in Year Two of 24, up from 18. The increase is healthy, and the degree of inequality remains pretty constant.

Then there is Option C, the least equitable in Year One, but presumably the one most directly correlated to retention of one's own output. It produced a Year Two total output of 25, the most significant jump. Note also that the least-well-off member in Year Two, Option C jumped from 4 to 7. So the least-well-off member of society now has 7 in each of three scenarios! Suddenly the distribution in "C" in Year One—the most inequitable and least appealing when viewed as a static matter—doesn't look so barbaric. Because by Year Two the least-well-off member has made the greatest strides, the least-well-off is at a par with the least well-off-members in the other distributive models, and the total wealth of the nation—25—is higher than in the other models! If this trend were to continue in Year Three and beyond, it might quickly outpace Options A and B. Indeed, even a Rawlsian might have a tough time arguing for either Option A or B, *if* over time the incomes actually moved along that trend line in Option C.

But what if the distribution of income under Option C in Year Two were not 7, 8, 10, but were instead 3, 6, 14? The poor are getting poorer, the wealthy wealthier, the middle stagnant, and total output in Year Two—now 23—is actually below the output in Option A! This is actually more akin to what the data suggest has happened to our income distribution and our economy. As income distribution has grown less equitable, the rate of growth has slowed. And as we all know, unfortunately, middle-income earnings have stagnated while the number of folks in poverty has increased. It would seem to me very tough, in that case, to justify Option C instead of Option A. Option A's distribution in Year Two of 7, 8, 9—with a total of 24—is a whole lot more appealing to me than Option C's Year Two distribution of 3, 6, 14—with a total of 23.

So the moral—and political—dilemma is to choose among these possible distribution schemes in the context of our best understanding of how shifting the burdens of taxes actually affects growth. Needless to say, establishing that causation is much more complex than simply overlaying tax rates and growth trends and assuming causation. There are a hundred other variables at play, and simply assuming that there is a causal relationship might itself be a flawed assumption.

Hence the enormous argument we have had about the actual impact tax rates will have on the wealthy. Do higher marginal rates inhibit growth and hard work from the "job creators"—as Paul Ryan, Mitt Romney, and Nozick might argue? Or do higher marginal rates raise revenue that permits investment by government that then leads to greater growth and equity as leading democrats and the progressive community would argue?

The learning on this seems pretty clear: There is little or no evidence that moving marginal rates up as has been proposed by the White House, or even slightly more by progressive voices, would have any negative impact on output by the wealthiest in our society. A recent study by the Congressional Research Service found without ambiguity that "this report attempts to clarify whether or not there is an association between the tax rates of the highest income taxpayers and economic growth. ... Analysis of such data suggests the reduction in the top tax rates have had little association with saving, investment, or productivity growth. However, the top tax rate reductions appear to be associated with the increasing concentration of income at the top of the income distribution."

The report continued:

> "The fitted values seem to suggest that higher tax rates are associated with slightly higher real per capita GDP growth rates. The top marginal tax rate in the 1950s was over 90%, and the real GDP growth rate averages 4.2% and real per capita GDP increased an-

nually by 2.4% in the 1950s. In the 2000s, the top marginal tax rate was 35% while the average real GDP growth rate was 1.7% and real per capita GDP increased annually by less than 1%.

"The scattered points, however, generally are not close to the fitted values line indicating that the association between GDP growth and the top tax rates is not strong. Furthermore, the observed positive association between real GDP growth and the top tax rates shown in the figure could be coincidental or spurious because of changes to the U.S. economy over the past 65 years. The statistical analysis using multivariate regression [...] does not find that either top tax rate has a statistically significant association with the real GDP growth rate."

It is perhaps no coincidence that the Republican leadership tried to have this report suppressed.

Stated in a different way, when you overlay the growth rates of our economy and the marginal tax rates that applied to the top earners, you see that there appears to be no correlation between lower rates and greater growth. None.

In fact, growth was at its highest when marginal rates were also at their highest. For a fascinating history of the debate surrounding our tax code, take a look at Steve Weisman's *The Great Tax Wars*. It sounds dry but isn't. It recounts the decades of controversy over many issues, including the one at the heart of today's debate: Where do increased marginal rates become counterproductive by actually inhibiting economic activity as opposed to generating additional revenue?

If one truly believes that higher marginal rates on the wealthy do not create a disincentive to work, and that increasing the burden of paying for government on the wealthy is a philosophically appropriate step, then moving rates up—as Presidents Clinton and Obama did—is the appropriate move. If, on the other hand, one believes that higher rates create an enormous disincentive, and that consequently the trajectory of growth from Year One to Year Two will be more akin to Option B, then higher rates are to be frowned upon, whether or not one believes in Rawls or Nozick.

As you can see, the issue can't be resolved without some mix of philosophy and data. Yet for all the high octane and high decibel screaming about our tax code, we rarely view it dispassionately—or through these prisms. We rarely ask ourselves the appropriate questions to determine what answer we want, based on our philosophical, moral, or economic analysis.

My sense is that most of us would be torn between the Rawlsian concern for the least-well-off and the Nozick concept that the fruits of hard work should be retained by those who produce. At the end of the day, the critical data, it seems to me, is that which suggests that higher marginal rates will not diminish output and future growth. If one adds to that the critical premise, which I accept, that only growth over the long term can indeed lift all boats, then some form of Option A—progressive tax rates and a social safety net geared toward increasing equality—makes sense.

What other polices are implicated by this vision of our social contract, if it is where we end up?

Consider our minimum wage laws. Even though a market for labor without a minimum wage might permit—or indeed drive—wages below the current statutory limit, we have a shared belief that those who are working full time should earn at least enough to pay for basic subsistence needs. (Of course, whether the current minimum wage law does that is open to question.) We have woven this belief into our legal framework. While there is also a pure economic argument that without the consumption power created by raising the minimum wage there would be not be a sufficient market for many goods, the more powerful argument for the minimum wage has always been the moral and philosophical. This reflects our shared agreement about the social contract we have embraced.

Indeed, perhaps the most important and emotionally gratifying cases we did while I was Attorney General were the minimum wage cases, where we were able to recover significant wages for a diverse group of workers who were being illegally underpaid. The group included deliverymen for supermarkets as well as waiters and bathroom attendants at high-end restaurants.

But perhaps the issue that best focuses the debate about our social contract is the inheritance tax. It stands as the gateway between those who simply, by virtue of birth, will begin with enormous advantages and wealth—a result of no work, aptitude, or moral argument on their own—and everybody else. The inequity that arises when viewed from the perspective of one who has no inheritance versus one who is the beneficiary of a significant inheritance is huge. Hence the belief many hold that the most morally and economically justifiable manner to raise government revenue is through an inheritance tax.

But two questions are necessary: First, does an inheritance tax in any way limit the productivity of those still alive? Does the desire to earn more—to be able to leave it to one's heirs—provide an important incentive for those still here? And would a confiscatory inheritance tax, as a consequence, again limit the growth potential of our economy? The short answer is we do not know the answer to this question. Phrased differently, would an inheritance tax—and at what levels—shift us in Year Two from Option C to Option A, or even Option B, in the differing growth models we suggested up above?

And secondarily, is an inheritance tax an unfair form of double taxation? Presumably the wealth that is subject to an inheritance tax has already been taxed once—when earned—under our current taxing structure. (To the extent that the income was never taxed, we are dealing with a loophole that needs to be closed, not the issue of an inheritance tax.)

As an intellectual matter, the inheritance tax is perhaps the sharpest point in the debate: It confronts the transference of wealth without any clear philosophical claim on the part of the recipient, and so the area where the argument for a higher tax is most appealing—unless it will substantially reduce the effort of those who truly generate wealth! My conclusion is that the inheritance tax can and should be raised—for both philosophical and economic reasons.

However you decide to answer these questions, this discussion is designed to set before you at a slightly more philosophical level the way we should think about how we structure our social contract, our tax code, and the benefit programs that redistribute wealth. From Social Security, to funding early education and Medicaid, the programs we have created should fit into a coherent philosophical structure. Of course they rarely do, and indeed they are generally a consequence of raw politics playing out at different moments in time.

To conclude on an affirmative note, I am of the view that the 2012 presidential election was actually a pretty good proxy contest for this debate. Surely, President Obama and Governor Romney did not invoke philosophical metaphors in their debates, yet the conversation was really one that contrasted two differing philosophical world views. Think about the question: Who built that? Was the world the one of Nozick where credit for "building it" was exclusively in the hands of the individual, and hence that individual had a moral claim to retain his earnings; or were we in a world of Rawls where we are concerned for those at the bottom and have the latitude to tax those who are better off without encumbering future growth and the prospects of future generations? Have those at the top derived their success because of their own hard work and ingenuity—or were they also lucky, fortunate to have inherited income and wealth? And, just as important, was Elizabeth Warren's comment—one I surely believe—that the great individual entrepreneurs nonetheless need the social infrastructure, from schools, to roads, to railways, upon which to build their companies.

Romney constantly invoked the language of job creators and rewarding those who produce, and derided the 47 percent who he said merely take without paying. In opposition stood Obama's invocation of a more communitarian perspective on the creation of wealth, a desire to focus on the hard-working yet not-yet-so-successful middle class, and a belief that those at the top can pay slightly more without impairing growth.

Beneath the partisanship and rancor of our politics, we were really all participating in a high-minded philosophical debate. Although I find the data pretty persuasive that the Obama worldview is correct, and the Rawlsian philosophical argument is compelling to me, I hope that, as we continue this debate, we all are willing to admit that the opposing views are at a minimum not without a certain intellectual coherence.

NOTES

1. Given the scope and nature of the investigation, I wasn't surprised when they responded through a phalanx of well-paid lawyers—led by the *former* Attorney General of the State of New York.

2. There was actually more than one bad actor in the subprime lending arena, but we focused on the worst in the New York market and tried to use our limited government resources to set a new standard.

3. The only exception was a conversation I had with Rudy Giuliani. Just as we were in court filing our injunction papers, he called from a Texas airport, saying he had just been retained by Merrill, and asserting that we really did not understand either the evidence or the industry. I assured him that in many conversations with Merrill's numerous lawyers we had been over all the issues at play. Oddly, he never re-emerged. I always presumed he had been retained in a last-ditch effort just to forestall our filing the case.

4. The NYSE's board consisted of five categories of directors: (1) insiders, such as Grasso and his subordinates, (2) specialists, (3) executives of securities firms other than specialists, (4) executives of firms listed on the NYSE, and (5) independent directors. As chairman and CEO of the NYSE, Grasso held significant power over not just insiders, but the specialists and executives of securities firms and listed firms as well. A specialist's income depends on the stocks that are assigned to him and how vigorously the Exchange's regulations governing specialists are enforced. As CEO of the NYSE, Grasso was in a position to significantly influence both of these factors. Similarly, executives of securities firms other than specialists were subject to Grasso's influence because they were heavily regulated by the NYSE. Directors who crossed Grasso could find themselves or their firms subject to intense regulatory scrutiny. Even listed companies could be helped or harmed by the influence Grasso held over the specialist responsible for the company's stock.

For example, in 2001, Maurice Greenberg, who was the chairman and CEO of AIG and a member of the NYSE's compensation committee, called Grasso to complain that the specialist in AIG stock was not doing enough to keep the stock price high. Grasso dutifully relayed Greenberg's concerns to the specialist in question, creating pressure to prop up the stock price. Similarly, when the National Association of Securities Dealers charged Ken Langone's trading firm with wrongdoing in April 2003, Grasso promptly called the head of the National Association of Securities Dealers on Langone's behalf.

5. In fact, even as Grasso sought an immediate payout of his SERP as part of his 2003 contract, Langone sought to conceal its size from the board. Notes from an October 2002 meeting of the compensation committee stated that "The Committee does not want to disclose to the full board the dollar value of the lump sum SERP benefit, so the Committee Chairman [Langone] is likely to use general terms in describing the Committee's deliberations in an effort to minimize conversation on the matter by the full Board."

In February 2003, after many directors had expressed shock at the size of Grasso's accumulated SERP and the consultants hired by the compensation committee to provide an independent review of Grasso's contract proposal informed Langone on two occasions that it did not appear that the committee appreciated the size of Grasso's SERP, Langone nonetheless proceeded to recommend a compensation award for Grasso that further increased his SERP without disclosing that information to the board.

And in March 2003, Langone asked the NYSE's attorney whether he could continue to withhold the amount of Grasso's SERP from the board, even as he sought board approval for the $140 million payout.

6. While Grasso and others have argued that this comparison was justified by the NYSE's role as a regulator of the financial industry, the fact is that, other than Dick Grasso, top executives of governmental or quasi-governmental regulatory organizations typically earn far less compensation than their private-sector counterparts. For example, from 1999 to 2002, the period during which Grasso earned more than $20 million per year (not counting the $80 million from his SERP), the chairman of the Federal Reserve Board, Alan Greenspan, received $172,000 per year, and the head of the Securities and Exchange Commission was paid $143,000 per year.

7. The Webb report also found that "Grasso's excessive compensation and benefits were the product of multiple flaws in the compensation and benefits process employed by the NYSE," including (a) the failure to adequately design, monitor, and oversee Grasso's SERP benefits; (b) faulty mechanics used to determine Grasso's yearly compensation; (c) lack of appropriate involvement of consultants in connection with Grasso's compensation and benefits; (d) lack of transparency regarding compensation; (e) lack of continuity and dedication on the compensation committee and board; and (f) Grasso's control over the people and processes that determine his compensation. Finally, the Webb report concluded that "Grasso's excessive levels of compensation and benefits... negatively affected the NYSE" from a financial and reputational standpoint.

8. *Id.* at 229.

9. I have avoided writing in this book about the ongoing litigation against Hank Greenberg, the former CEO of AIG. Because the case is still pending, I think it better that I limit my comments. That notwithstanding, several points must be made, given the constant effort to rewrite history. (It might be worth looking at my appearance on CNBC with Maria Bartiromo on July 13, 2012.)

Here are a few salient and irrefutable points:

1. AIG and Hank Greenberg were charged by the New York Attorney General's office—when I was Attorney General—with civil fraud and deceptive accounting practices, as well as a raft of other abuses;

2. AIG settled those charges for $1.64 billion, at the time the largest payment in history. *The New York Times* reported the settlement as follows:

"Under the settlement reached with the Justice Department, the Securities and Exchange Commission, the New York attorney general's office, and the New York State Insurance Department, A.I.G. acknowledged that it had deceived the investing public and regulators."

3. Further from *The Times*:

"Mr. Greenberg, who was removed by A.I.G.'s board last March, remains under investigation by the Securities and Exchange Commission and the Justice Department and faces a lawsuit by the New York attorney general, Eliot Spitzer."

4. A quote from a Bloomberg News report about the removal of Greenberg by the board:

"Last night, AIG announced that Greenberg, 79, would step down as chief executive officer. ... Greenberg's resignation as CEO came as New York Attorney General Eliot Spitzer zeroed in on a specific reinsurance transaction between AIG and Berkshire Hathaway Inc.'s General Reinsurance subsidiary. ... Spitzer obtained information in the past 10 to 14 days that Greenberg himself may have initiated the transaction..."

5. Lest there be ANY doubt about the veracity of this claim of Greenberg's role, here is a quote from a federal judge's written opinion after a federal criminal prosecution that focused on these very transactions:

"The government presented sufficient evidence that, starting with Greenberg's October 31 2000 phone call to Ferguson, there was an agreement to carry out a transaction to artificially inflate AIG's loss reserves and deceive investors about the amount of the company's loss reserves and quality of earnings." More from the federal judge: "The evidence provides an adequate basis for a rational jury to conclude that the conspiracy to artificially inflate AIG's loss reserves and deceive the company's investors started with Greenberg's call to Ferguson on October 31, 2000."

6. Perhaps that is why Greenberg invoked his Fifth Amendment right to avoid answering questions when we invited him to explain these transactions.

7. And perhaps that is why after the SEC and the Justice Department charged him in 2009 for the actions relating to these same transactions; he settled for $15 million.

8. Greenberg was deemed to be an unindicted co-conspirator by federal prosecutors, invoked his Fifth Amendment right to avoid answering questions, and was removed by his own board of directors after the accounting at AIG was deemed to be unreliable. Our case against him was rock solid.

CPSIA information can be obtained at www.ICGtesting.com
Printed in the USA
LVOW06s1732140813

347904LV00007B/802/P